The New Nuns

The New Nuns

SERVING WHERE THE SPIRIT LEADS

John Deedy

Fides/Claretian

For Carroll T. Dozier, Bishop of Memphis,
Inspiration, and confidant, since Norfolk

ISBN 0-8190-0649-1
Cover design: Glenn Heinlein
Cover art: A. A. Chatelin
LC 82-11895
First printing, August 1982

Fides/Claretian books are a series of books, published by
the Claretian Fathers and Brothers, which examine the
issue of Christian social justice in the United States.
The books are written for grassroots Christians seeking
social justice. They are based on the premise that it is
not possible for everyone to do everything, but it is a
Christian duty for everyone to do something.

For further information about Fides/Claretian, write to
the address below.

221 West Madison Street • Chicago. Illinois 60606

Contents

Contents

Part III

Foreword

Several weeks ago, in a state hospital in Chicago where I've worked for the past two years, a patient who described himself as once an order priest asked me: "Are you a liberal nun?" I smiled. (I'd been wondering how a 48-year-old father of six feels as he waits in neurosurgery to discover why he's losing control of his body.) I didn't answer his question. I listened instead as he told me how he'd argued a reluctant priest into baptizing a friend's baby "Carroll," how he loves his lesbian daughter though he disapproves of her lifestyle, how he lives poorly and is hopeful that someday his children will understand the reason. The conversation was interrupted when doctors making rounds appeared in the doorway.

It is 20 years since *The Nun in the World* by Cardinal Leon Joseph Suenens was distributed in Rome during the closing hours of the first session of Vatican II, and still nuns mystify the world. Suenens proposed in 1962 a theology of apostolic life for religious which questioned "traditional" enclosure, garb, activities, place in the church, and presence to the world of nuns as we knew them. His analysis provoked controversy, which American sisters broadened and deepened while they studied the Council documents and prepared their chapters in the light of the vision of the People of God reflecting on the signs of their times. Out of their experience they began to fashion a new life and new rules for their communities, to better express their origins. The process continued as an anguishing church looked on. While aware of losing "the good sister," it was traumatized by the departure of thousands of nuns and priests from official ministry.

John Deedy narrates the passage from 1962 to 1982 through the lives of certain new nuns. I am grateful for the objectivity an outsider brings to this epic of survival and transformation. *The New Nuns, Serving Where the Spirit Leads* continues for me the story we tried to tell in *Women in Ministry: A Sisters' View* (1972) and *Gospel Dimensions of Ministry* (1973). It is the most recent volume of this work in process, the coming-of-age of women religious and their congregations in the U.S. I consider it a step forward that the book is written by a man and published professionally. Ten years ago, when women religious were struggling desperately to escape from the status of minors in the church, our resources were so few that we had to write, edit, and finance the communications we wished dispatched to the world.

How did the nuns break into the modern world? Each sister has her own version of the slow, difficult, costly journey, which continues to open new horizons daily. John Deedy mentions several historical factors, like nuns' involvement in the civil-rights' marches, the Vietnam protests, the efforts of women's lib. I find traces in his book of an experience that I believe cut deeper into the consciousness of religious, enabling them to claim space and a new identity in the world. I refer to the sisters' movement.

Given the pressures in the church demanding that we conform, that we not jeopardize our communities' relations with local clergy and the hierarchy, we sisters needed peers with whom to share our hopes, dreams, and the risk of bringing something unknown into being. The coming together of sisters open to a changing world, who discovered one another across congregational lines, is the event that changed for me the reality of what religious life could become.

Sisters who spent time together on campuses and at summer institutes, who planned renewal days for their congregations and shared ideas about formation experiments, provided the creative energies and commitment that gave birth to local and national groups whose goal was to change the face of the earth and church. Between the late 1960s and mid-1970s more than a hundred diocesan councils or senates came into existence. During the same period, to support the broader and more complicated issues that preoccupied nuns, grassroots groups were formed around the National Coalition of American Nuns, National Assembly of Women Religious, National Black Sisters Conference, Association of Contemplative Sisters, Las Hermanas, Network, and possibly others I have forgotten. NCAN, NAWR, NBSC, and ACS carried the voice of sisters on the move to major superiors, bishops, priests, brothers, and laity, through headlines in religious and secular press when face-to-face encounters were not achievable. Gradually our concerns moved beyond the boundaries of the church, to the poor who cried out for justice. In the process the earlier distinction of grassroots sister and leadership person became blurred. We formed coalitions to bring our initiatives and their resources together.

Foreword

I know no one who has tried to measure the influence of the sisters' movement on American nuns. We who were there in the beginning, however, will remember always how it engaged us beyond our hopes, strengths, and imagining and created a forum for developing relationships with the world beyond the reach of contemporary church experience. Confrontations and compromises on the floor of conventions, facing the media, 24-hour days for strategy and action converted a "prophetic" handful of religious into a leavening group of new nuns. No wonder Deedy refuses to categorize the type as a passing phenomenon.

There is nostalgia even among new nuns for an era that is gone, when a convention speaker would address 2000 sisters. Are there any issues that can gather more than a few hundred sisters, when prayer vigils in New York and Chicago to protest the murder of four women missionaries in El Salvador assembled no more? Probably not, at least not by themselves. The movement perhaps has completed its task. Nuns are in the world, immersed in responding to the needs of people to whom they have committed themselves—at least many of them are. As I listened to John Deedy's interviews, I felt a stability, realism, and inner strength in these new nuns that reminded me of biblical women; they no longer need numbers because the Word has taken flesh among them.

A few words of appreciation for the new from the old. Whatever the age, culture, ministry, presence in church or secular structure, they speak to me of singleminded dedication to and identification with those to whom they minister. Was it as evident in us, years ago, when so much of our energy was spent trying to lay foundations for dialogue and decision making in the church? We felt we didn't know when our time would run out.

The new nuns' present is a future they planned; they studied, reflected about, and researched their project. In the 1970s we were so often generalists. We grabbed insights on the run and translated them into action plans for yesterday.

They've made history by creating and functioning in nontraditional roles or developing new models for traditional ministeries that are being abandoned. They provide a precedent others may choose to follow. We strove for the right to shape history, having few to rely on even within our congregations.

If, as Deedy suggests, the ordination of women to the priesthood is only a matter of time, that the church must one day open ministries equally to men and women, then surely the labors of the new nuns are advancing the hour.

SISTER ETHNE KENNEDY, S.H.

Introduction

First off, let me anticipate a reader objection. What is a man doing writing a book about the New Nun? Doesn't the arrangement smack of sexism, male usurpation of a topic that better belongs in the hands of a woman? Couldn't Fides/Claretian have found a woman writer to do a book on the so-called New Nun?

I encountered the objection in my research and interviewing, and I can appreciate aspects of it. War books, certainly in their gory dimension, are books for men— male writers: Stephen Crane, Erich Maria Remarque, James Jones. (Oooops! Did someone bring up the name of Margaret Mitchell?) Conversely, books about nuns might best be written by persons who share the gender, whether they be nuns, ex-nuns, Catholic, whatever. One of the most useful books to me in my research was *The Nuns,* a report on modern women religious—who they are, what they do, how they live in a world of future shock. It was written by Marcelle Bernstein. She is Jewish.

That noted, let it now be said that Fides/Claretian approached three women about their doing this book. The three declined, for a variety of reasons, some understandable. I was approached. I said yes, but with hesitation. I was sensitive to the notion that so feminist a topic might be best handled by a woman. If nothing more, it seemed the more politic course.

On the other hand I figured that, if I did not share the gender, I did share some necessary sensibilities, and I did have a credential or two for writing and interviewing on the subject. I wasn't exactly a stranger to the theme of the New Nun.

When a dozen New York-area nuns disrupted a Cardinal Cooke Mass in St. Patrick's Cathedral one spring Sunday in 1972, prostrating themselves in the cathedral's center aisle in protest over Catholic apathy on the Vietnam war, the *New York Times* asked me to write of the witness of the nuns and the implications of their actions, which I did for its "Week in Review" section. It was the first of the dramatic assertions—or at least the most dramatic of the early assertions on the part of the New Nun, and the *Times* was fascinated and curious. It sensed that something radical was occurring in the hitherto placid world of women religious.

Indeed something truly radical *had* occurred, and the incident in St. Patrick's Cathedral pointed up the fact. This was no intramural squabble, no small institutional fight, such as a group of nuns being in contention with an archbishop or the Vatican over a change in garb or a modification of an apostolate. The incident dramatized that the story went much deeper, that the whole concept of women's religious life had perhaps changed, and maybe the sisterhoods themselves.

The rest of the media became as intrigued as the *Times* with the story, and soon the headline became a commonplace: "You've Come a Long Way, Sister," a play obviously on the popular cigarette commercial, "You've come a long way, baby." The *Times'* headline on my story was "Sisters Have Come a Long Way," a bit stodgy but then the *Times'* style has always leaned towards the formal.

Incidentally, those protesting sisters were not prosecuted. They were dragged from the cathedral by ushers and police and taken to the East 51st Street station, where seven were booked on charges of interfering with a religious service, and served summonses for a court appearance two weeks hence. The Archdiocese of New York, however, did not press court charges, thus showing admirable good judgment. The archdiocese was in a no-win situation, and to have prosecuted the nuns would have been to cast itself in the role of ogre.

So I was a part of the early media exploration of the New Nun story. Several years later, when *ICI*, the esteemed Parisian monthly, devoted a special issue to women religious of the world and the *profond renouveau* they had undergone since Vatican Council II, it was I who was asked to do the article on nuns of the *Etats-Unis*. It appeared in the issue of November, 1979. All of which is said by way of overcoming objections to my authorship of this book.

Passing on, the reader will note that I am using the words nun and sister interchangeably. There is, of course, a distinct ecclesiastical difference of meaning between the two words. Traditionally the word nun has defined one in solemn vows, such as a contemplative or one living in an enclosed group. The word sister has applied to a woman in simple vows. Generally she belonged to "active orders," such as teaching or nursing communities, or other communities whose works were carried on outside the convent or enclosure. At one time a careful distinction was made in the use of the two words, but no longer. Nun and sister have become virtual synonyms for one another, and they are so used in this book.

One other point to be made early on is that I do not use the term New Nun in reference to age. In my research I encountered women in their seventies who were as swinging, if that is an allowable word in the context, as any of the new breed of nun. I also encountered very young nuns who were old in the sense of being right out of the mold that produced the parochial school teacher of my early education back in the 1930s. So the term New Nun is really used to identify an apostolic type rather than an age or generational group.

I should add that it is used also to identify an attitudinal type, for the New Nun, as my interviews should make abundantly clear, has dispositions, manners, feelings, positions, lifestyles that break dramatically with the recent (if not historical) past. The New Nun is in the mold of her historical antecedents, but somewhere along the line sisters became institutionalized and so reclusive that the reversion to roles that were hers make it seem almost as if a new species of religious had suddenly appeared in the evolutionary development of the person of religion. This was not the case. The New Nun is in the mold of the Original Nun. Mercy Sister Theresa Kane, for instance, was not the first nun to lecture a pope. Another Theresa—Teresa of Avila—did too, and she won canonization. Catherine of Siena is a better example.

Whether the New Nun is an American phenomenon I do not presume to say. My hunch is that what is happening in the sisterhoods in the United States is but a reflection of much that is occurring elsewhere, notably in Latin America. But, as I say, that is only a hunch. It is for others to explore the wider implications.

I should say something about the interviewees of the book. I did not seek out persons of particular ideological stripe. I looked rather for sisters who were in interesting and possibly inspiring apostolates. Their ecclesial and political ideology I discovered only in the course of our conversations. In other words I did not go searching for people with a cause. I went looking for women of devout dedication to a work which in some way departed from the more traditional apostolates of the woman religious. For example, instead of searching out a sister who has a ministry in prisons, a type I knew and publicized as far back as the 1950s, I sought out a sister who runs a halfway house for women coming out of prison. Instead of interviewing a sister who works in Catholic Charities, I turned to one who had given up a high school principalship to work among the poor of Appalachia. Instead of interviewing the standard (and often heroic) parochial school teacher, I chose two sisters who run a grade school which accents values rather than religion. If the New Nun may be categorized as a class or group, these are the new nuns.

What should be obvious is that I have not sought out famous personalities for the interviews. All my subjects are anonymous, or relatively so, so far as the media spotlight is concerned. There is no Sister Theresa Kane among them. This was done quite purposefully. I hate the word grassroots, but sisters in the grassroots were precisely whom I wanted to explore, not those like Theresa Kane who stand tall in the new growth. I wanted to probe who the New Nun was, what motivated her, how she felt about things. Mine is not a scientific probe by any means, but it does, I trust, reveal some important and challenging information.

The reader will note that certain questions were asked of all or several of the nuns—for instance, their feelings about their earlier careers as sisters; their feelings about the ordination of women; their feelings about male clerical structures in the church. The reason for this was to explore how widely opinions extended on matters that touched all sisters. I do not lay claim to any hard sociological conclusions on the basis of answers to those questions, but it is astonishing how many answers fell into a single pattern. The reader will discover this in the reading.

Sometimes it may seem that the interviewees were rehearsed by one another or selectively chosen by the interviewer. They were not. Each of the sisters interviewed was allowed to review the transcript of her interview tape, but only in order to check the accuracy of my editing and in a few instances the reassembling of thoughts. Not one sought to make a substantive change in the transcript; not one pleaded that she had "misspoke"—that marvelous word that the Nixon Administration gave the language. At that point I had in mind the oral-history approach. Subsequently I adopted a narrative style in the interest of having a more readable book. I rewrote from the transcripts. These pages were not reviewed by the sisters.

One last thing: The title of this book is not exactly novel. Sister M. Charles Borromeo Muckenhirn edited a symposium-type book, which carried the title *The New Nuns*. That was back in 1967. It was a useful book, and it shed light on new directions in the sisterhoods. But it was still so early in the sisterhoods' Vatican II renewal process that no single essay was devoted to the women's-ordination question. In any instance I resurrect the title and claim it for this book and the nuns 15 years removed from Muckenhirn's. That's only half a generation, as time is measured. But today's nun is a new breed. She is the end result of Vatican II and its Constitution on the Church in the Modern World. In its own way the Constitution on the Church in the Modern World was the "bread-and-butter" document of the Council, since it dealt not only with the world, but the world in the most specific of senses. No group in the church took this document more seriously than women religious. In instance after instance they have made the modern world theirs, finding the modern world good—or correctable. It is what makes the New Nun in the modern world a fascinating and inspiring creature.

Part I

Back on the Cutting Edge

In 1966, the year after the close of Vatican Council II, there were 182,000 nuns in the United States. In 1981 their number was down to 122,600, a decline of 31 percent in a period of 15 years. This is a percentage decline exceeding that of nuns worldwide. Worldwide the drop in nuns for the same period was roughly 25 percent.

The decline in nuns is a phenonemon which no one anticipated during those heady Council years. Yet it occurred, and with such precipitousness in the United States as to work large and seemingly permanent handicaps on numerous aspects of institutional Catholicism. At the very least it was responsible for the changing of certain institutional patterns. Many parochial schools had to close for want of sisters to teach in them—academies and colleges, too. Some hospitals had to be turned over to community organizations or private groups, again because of a shortage of sisters to manage and staff them. Other apostolates have similarly suffered, such as parish Confraternity of Christian Doctrine programs. Dedicated laity have stepped into the latter apostolic breach, but it is obvious that the sisters are sorely missed.

On the surface the situation in the sisterhoods would

appear to be one of crisis, of rout, of demoralization. But quite the opposite is the case. The sisterhoods have their problems, to be sure. The departure rate has abated considerably, but some still leave, older nuns die, and there are not enough new vocations to gain against the losses. Nevertheless it is among women religious that some of the most exhilarating activities are taking place in the American Catholic Church, and it is among women religious that one finds the spirit of the post-Vatican II church most vibrant. When Vatican II issued *Perfectae caritatis*, the Decree on the Appropriate Renewal of the Religious Life, the sisterhoods responded with immediacy and enthusiasm. And faster than any other element of the church, the sisters assimilated the other 15 documents of the Council.

Indeed it is a totally new day for the American nun, and, to the extent that it is fair to generalize, she herself is a totally new person. Gone completely is the stereotype of the American nun as the last of the unliberated species of American womanhood, a person moving about in antique garb, speaking only when spoken to, detached from the activist life, and subservient in almost humiliating measure to the male authority line of the church. Today's nun is no Ingrid Bergman playing Sister Benedict to Bing Crosby's Father O'Malley in some kind of real-life version of "The Bells of St. Mary's." Today's nuns are mature and independent in ways they never were before, and they carry a heightened consciousness of themselves as women and as Catholics. They move freely and self-assuredly in ecclesiastical and secular society, many of them on their own terms so far as work, hours, dress, and living arrangements are concerned. They are confident, outspoken, activist, and less beholden to Father. Mercy Sister M.

Theresa Kane of the Leadership Conference of Women Religious may not have been precisely typical of the New Nun, when she admonished Pope John Paul II during his 1979 American visit on the equal role that should be women's "in all ministries of our church." But she certainly demonstrated the independence which characterizes the New Nun, and she testified that human rights must apply as fully to the sisterhoods, as to any other segment of people, society, or church.

Of course traditional strains survive in the church— nuns, for instance, who prefer the old ways and the traditional apostolates. One must be grateful for these nuns, for there is still much teaching, nursing, and missionary work to be done. Most of the old apostolates retain their validity, however hobbled some might be these days because of shortages of women religious. Further, it is quite possible to be a so-called New Nun in an old apostolate, for the New Nun is a state of mind as much as it is a change of habit, in the vocational as well as the stylistic sense. The New Nun welcomes her upgraded role as a religious, her broader latitudes, her improved freedoms, and she appears determined on expanding her gains. Most emphatically she rejects her former lot, real or imagined, as being something of "a cheap labor force" to do the bishop's work or Father's will. Respectfully as possible, the New Nun is resolved to be her own person.

The New Nun was not born overnight. Several forces, some religious, some secular, gave thrust to her development. There was even a far-away push by Pope Pius XII, who by 1948 was telling religious superiors to adapt or perish.

Certainly the New Nun evolved in major part out of

13

Vatican II with its conciliar emphases on religious freedom and the dignity of the person, both as a human right,
personal and collective. The emphases were spelled out in
the Declaration on Religious Freedom. Father John
Courtney Murray, S.J., architect of the declaration, saw
clearer than the Council Fathers the implications of the
declaration. "Inevitably," he said, "a second great argu-
ment will be set afoot—now on the theological meaning of
Christian freedom." For, as he noted, those who receive
this freedom "assert it within the church as well as within
the world." The sisterhoods were not exempt from Murray's prediction. In fact some of the most fascinating and
controversial assertions of religious freedom were to occur
among nuns.

Secular forces helping shape the New Nun included the
civil-rights movement of the 1960s and the antiwar movement of the late 1960s, early 1970s. Both drew the nun out
of her convent and thrust her into direct contact with a
new world of issues, issues from which she had been
walled off before and which now caught her up emo-
tionally and spiritually. Also, there was "women's lib," the
women's liberation movement, and in legislative circles the
struggle for passage of an Equal Rights Amendment to the
Constitution; nothing quickened the consciousness of
women as women more than "women's lib" and the fight
for ERA. This was true for women in convents as much as
for women in kitchens. The sisterhoods do not exist in a
vacuum. Assertions by feminists on behalf of a totally just
and equitable society could not be expected to leave sisters
and the sisterhoods themselves untouched. A quickened
consciousness of woman's place in the general society

could only produce a new consciousness about sister's place in the society of her church.

And so the New Nun was born, although not suddenly and not in immediately large numbers. It was only a relatively few nuns, for instance, who joined in the Freedom Rides and who stood in the front ranks in Selma and Birmingham against the police dogs and the water cannons of the racist establishment. By the same token it was a solitary nun, a Religious of the Sacred Heart of Mary—Elizabeth McAlister, later to become the wife of former Josephite Father Philip Berrigan—who dramatized that outrage over the Vietnam War reached into the convents of America. But the involvement of a few became the commitment of many, and soon there were scores of nuns in civil-rights demonstrations and scores more in the streets protesting the war and, after the war, the nuclear arms race. Thus it was that when McAlister came to trial in Harrisburg in 1972 on charges of conspiracy against the United States government, testimony revealed that she was far from being a lonesome religious. Her "accomplices" included nuns who acted as mail drops for letters that moved between Berrigan, then in prison, and McAlister, then still in the convent. The New Nun was a distinct reality. Soon scores became hundreds, and hundreds became thousands, and these nuns helped turn tides against racism, against the war, against travesties of freedom and human dignity. In the course of all this the New Nun looked at her church and sensed that it was not the perfect society either. So were initiated actions that would make the church a better institution and one more aware of its female elements.

Back on the Cutting Edge

Life for American nuns is quite different today from what it was just a decade ago, even for traditionalist types. Habits have been modernized, rules have been relaxed, even among those who carry on historic apostolates in familiar settings—teaching in parochial schools, nursing in hospitals, staffing homes for the handicapped and the aged, serving in missions in foreign lands. But the point is this: The sister one recognizes from yesterday is not the sum of the sisterhoods today. Another breed of nuns has evolved, nuns unconstrained by old conventions and free to take part in a widened social apostolate. These nuns are encountered in drug and alcoholic rehabilitation programs, in storefront missions in the ghettos, in migrant worker camps, campus ministries, in theological professorships in colleges and seminaries, in spiritual directorships, in pulpits as preachers of missions, at corporation meetings arguing issues of corporate responsibility.

They even can be encountered now in the halls of Congress as lobbyists for or against legislation affecting the human condition. They are there as members of Network, one of only two specifically Catholic lobbies working in the Congress, the other being the United States bishops' national conference. Network was started by sisters ten years ago, and although it is not an exclusively sisters' organization anymore, Network now being open to men and women of every calling, sisters continue to be its core community. The group is called Network because of the participants' system of "network-ing by telephone," of alerting sisters all over the country when certain legislative bills are coming up for hearing or for voting. The word speeds out from Washington to convents and sisters' apartments in the 50 states, and the sisters go into action as

16

a socio-political bloc, organizing letter-writing campaigns, telephoning, visiting the offices of their representative or senator for what might be called a little bit of arm twisting.

In sum, the New Nun can be found anywhere, and sometimes not even be recognized, for her identity as a religious may be nothing more than an inconspicuous cross or some other symbol. The New Nun is often not given to the wearing of the habit. Nor is she always given to convent life. It is not unusual, accordingly, to find many nuns living apart from their religious community in small groups of their own, in rooms or apartments, often next door to their work or those they serve, and thus more accessible to them in their need. Some of these nuns are subsidized by their order, some by a parish or an apostolate; some live on the wages of their labor as working nuns in the world.

Not everyone is happy about these developments. Pope John Paul II has spoken out several times against the shedding of the religious habit and against departures from formal religious modes. Cardinal Ildebrando Antoniutti of the Vatican's Congregation of Religious has commented that "in the army no one is allowed to choose his own uniform," therefore why should sisters be allowed to dress as they please? And as for nuns in the world, an American cardinal has remarked that "sisters who choose their own place of work are doing the work of the devil."

Such strong clerical remonstrances would one day have sent shock waves through orders of women religious. But not now. Women superiors are more independent and more tolerant about what their sisters do with their vocations. The New Nun thus goes about her mission not contemptuous of authority but confident in conscience and assured about her right to serve and to witness in manner other than what some male authority figure might think best for her. There has been no rush back to the habit, no procession back to the convent, no marked inclination to quit her new work for more formal apostolates of yesterday.

Not unexpectedly a certain antipathy may exist among some nuns maintaining the old ways towards those who are expressing their individuality in different, almost revolutionary fashion. But it is an antipathy that seems to be easily broken down with contact and by coming to an understanding that the world changes, the church changes, and so must the sisterhoods. The *New York Times* told not long ago of the bridging of old attitudes and new in the Dominican Sisters' community in Amityville, Long Island. Older retired nuns could not fully appreciate the decision of many younger nuns to engage in service apostolates that necessitated their living elsewhere. When they were young sisters, they stayed in their convents and they helped to look after the older sisters, making the beds, doing the cleaning and dusting, and performing whatever other tasks that were asked of them. Hostility and suspicion towards the New Nun disappeared, however, as the younger sisters returned for visits to the Amityville motherhouse and mixed with the older sisters, praying with them, playing with them, taking them on outings, as to beaches in the summer and to shopping malls for Christmas gift buying. One particular nun, it seems, presented more of a problem than the others for the older sisters. She came out from the city in slacks and was quite independent. Many of the older nuns were not sure how to take her. But after a few days of working hard in the garden and visiting, new

and old got to know one another, and one derived as much benefit from the contact as the other.

To the extent that disapproval of new apostolic lifestyles does exist, it has not swelled to any serious rifts among women religious communities. Some traditionalist sisters have grouped together in an organization called Consortium Perfectae Caritatis (Partnership of Perfect Charity), but there would seem to be as much room for them on the American religious landscape as there is for the Leadership Conference of Women Religious, which has official recognition by the Vatican, or the more militant National Coalition of American Nuns, to mention just two sisters' organizations. The male priesthood is not an ideological or religious monolith; the Catholic laity is not; there is no reason why the sisterhood should be.

If it is true that the New Nun has established a broader social role for herself in the modern world, it does not precisely follow that she has achieved what she would consider the ideal for herself in the modern church. To be sure, many American sisters are functioning in upgraded capacities in the church—as ministers of the Eucharist, as lectors and commentators at Mass, as members of liturgical commissions, as team members of parish ministries, as diocesan officials in high administrative posts, etc. Still, though their station has improved, the impression is common that their new roles are secondary ones and, as often as not, have come by default. In a word they result from the clergy drain and the decline in priestly vocations and not from a pure desire to involve women more significantly in the church's ministries.

Inevitably this situation feeds a certain cynicism. Sisters new and old prefer that their gains in the church stem from a positive, spontaneous appreciation of their worth as women and not because they are the convenient answer to some male personnel problem—"slot fillers," as it were. Pope and bishops would argue that this is an unfair reading of the situation, that women religious have always been appreciated, and that their elevated roles as religious derives less from need in the church body generally than from a Vatican II understanding of mission and service, and of the greater responsibilities all Catholics must assume in the affairs of God and church. The sentiment is uplifting, but the fact that almost every gain for women religious has followed a crisis of one sort or another leaves some people dubious about the absolute sincerity of the words.

For not a few sisters, and for the New Nun especially, the acid test of sincerity relates to the pastoral and sacramental ministries. Very many American nuns believe that their position in the church will be an inferior one until the last doors are opened to them, notably that of the priesthood itself. Admittedly, not all American nuns want to be ordained as priests. At the same time, however, until ordination is available to nuns at least as an option, many nuns will be convinced that they are second-class members of their church.

Several sisters' groups have pressured the bishops on the issue of ministry, and the bishops, in fairness to them, have not been as unresponsive as they have sometimes been portrayed. Several years ago the bishops set up an Ad Hoc Committee on Women in Society and in the Church, one of whose purposes is to put into effect "insofar as possible" those matters already agreed on by the body of bishops identifying, formally authenticating, and extending ministries performed by women in the church. The committee—comprising six bishops and five women consultors—first met in Chicago in April, 1979 with three representatives of the Women's Ordination Conference to discuss how they should approach issues and conduct dialogue. The committee came up with no instant solutions to problems, but that was less important at the embryo stage than the willingness just to sit down together and talk. In that limited respect the dialogue got off to a good start. Mercy Sister Elizabeth Carroll, a member of the core commission of the Women's Ordination Conference, termed those 1979 discussions "the most pleasant" she ever had with bishops. She credited the bishops with being "concerned about the needs of women" and receptive to "a climate in which dialogue is possible."

On June 3, 1981 the first concrete report was forthcoming. It summarized a year of discussion between the bishops' committee and representatives of the Women's Ordination Conference, and made the point that the exclusion of women from full participation in the church is a "serious matter" and may indeed be increasing alienation of women from the church. The dialogue covered the church's understanding of personhood, the nature of patriarchy, and how change is brought about in the church.

The report said that the participants reached "mutually acknowledged conclusions" without implying agreement. It did specify, however, that "we mutually agree that the alienation of women from the church is a serious pastoral problem." And in the section describing "conclusions mutually acknowledged" to be "serious matters," the participants said: "The many levels of exclusion of women from full participation in the church raise serious questions for

21

women regarding the extent to which the church effectively acknowledges the full human personhood of women
and their equal redemption in Christ." Those are land-
mark sentiments, however limited the authority of the participants to effect change.

Even those sentiments were sharpened a year later when
the bishops' committee, no longer ad hoc, issued a 13-page
report on further meetings with the Women's Ordination
Conference. Released April 27, 1982 the report recom-
mended that more church ministries, "perhaps including
the diaconate," be opened to women, and more as-
tonishingly called for review of the Vatican's 1976 declaration stating that women cannot be ordained priests. The
committee said that "a sexist attitude" is indeed pervasive
among members of the church and its leadership, and it
posed the question: "Does the hierarchical nature of the
church necessarily have to be patriarchal?" Copies of the
report were sent to all the bishops of the United States.

Another indication that American bishops—some at
least—are moving progressively on the matter of women
in the church was the awarding May 22, 1981 of the annual *U.S. Catholic* award for furthering women's cause in
the church to five bishops—the five actually being representative of the many who had acted decisively in their
dioceses and in the community at large in behalf of a more
just treatment of women in the church and in society. The
five were: Archbishop Raymond G. Hunthausen of Seat-
tle, Archbishop Rembert G. Weakland, O.S.B., of Milwaukee, retired Bishop Charles A. Buswell of Pueblo,
Colo., Bishop Michael McAuliffe of Jefferson City, Mo.,
and Bishop William E. McManus of Fort Wayne-South
Bend, Ind.

In presenting the award Rev. Mark J. Brummel, C.M.F., *U.S. Catholic* editor, cited the bishops for having spoken out, written, or otherwise taken steps to eliminate sexist language and references from the liturgy, for promoting affirmative action in their spheres of influence, for helping raise the awareness of others in the church about women's rights as Catholics, and for actually giving women a greater voice in church matters. Archbishop Hunthausen, for instance, was singled out for putting good words into action in his diocese by putting into practice the practical suggestions of his Pastoral Letter on Women, thus moving towards the goal of equality in diocesan affairs. "We are pleased to be able to honor five men—bishops at that—who have had such an effect on the role of women in the church," said Brummel. And indeed he had cause to be pleased. Five or ten years before, the award probably would have gone begging if the donor had gone looking in the direction of the episcopacy.

But, of course, dialogue even on a national level can lead only so far. The ultimate decisions on issues of substance are reserved to Rome, and most especially the issue of ordination of women. Rome is adamantly opposed to the idea of women priests, but there are those who believe that Rome cannot be forever adamant, that it must act soon and positively, or else risk an insitutional catastrophe so far as the church's sisterhoods are concerned. They argue that the future of the sisterhoods is bound up with ordination, and that unless the option of ordination exists for women the drain of women religious over the past 15 years will become a massive exodus in the 1980s.

One who believes this is Sister Margaret Ellen Traxler, S.S.N.D., director of the Institute of Women Today in Chicago and founder in 1969 of the National Coalition of American Nuns. "Women gathering together in community," she said, "should not have to submit to the oppression of a man who is not a member of the religious community and comes into the sanctuary to offer Mass while the obedient women must stay in the pews." The comment may have a tendentious tone to it, but it is born of a perception common to many in today's sisterhoods: "The very self-image of woman is abused in the present all-male clerical system."

Traxler is not afraid to speak out. "I often ask myself," she said, "if I want the exodus from religious life to continue. The response is in anguish, for if the male domination continues, the exodus will continue. Only those older nuns, of whom I number myself, can remember the suffering of teaching or serving in schools and hospitals where ignorant pastors and power-seeking bishops held control and oppressed in unbelievable ways. If that is the way of the future, then yes, I want that kind of religious life to end—and it will end no matter how we wish otherwise. So many clerics set themselves up as the ultimate critics of nuns, and they have never taken the vows of women or responded to those vows as women. They cannot know the pressures of servitude suffered by women at the hands of the all-male church network."

Traxler remarked that she hears nuns say, "I will no longer work for or within the institutional church." She declared that she hears the remark repeatedly. But she takes comfort, she commented, that the "growing consensus does not mean an end to service to the global community of church—for church is all of the people of the entire planet." What she means is that a sister's commitment to service can be as efficacious outside as well as inside the institutional church.

Not all agree that the ordination issue so dominates the psyche and the ambition of today's nun. "A deeper, harder question," said an article in *Sisters Today*, "is the development of a new church which would *actually* identify itself with the poor, the alienated, and the oppressed, a new church community developed and based in mutual relationships of service-ministries, of decision making, of responsibility." Whether this is indeed a "deeper, harder question" or rather a question of another sort with its own distinct category of importance is beside the point. The point is that it dramatizes the survival of the old idealisms in the current generations of nuns. Yesterday's nun most certainly helped the church identify with the poor, the oppressed, the alienated, and if she did not exactly remake the church, she did convey to it dimensions of concern and compassion vital to its spiritual and humanitarian mission. Today's nun, however politicized some of them and however independent many more, is in the apostolic tradition of her predecessor. Her concerns might find different expressions at times, but she is still a person uniquely dedicated to God and to humankind.

It should also be noted that the New Nun of strong feminist cast, prominent as she may be on the American religious scene, is not the sum of the modern American sisterhood. The old work goes on in its own quiet ways, often among people who are largely invisible to the rest of society. An inspiring example of this would be the Missionaries of Charity, members of Mother Teresa's order, who work in the South Bronx area of New York City. The South Bronx is a half-a-world away from India and

Bangladesh, where Mother Teresa's order is especially active, but it is close to both in terms of mission, serving "the poorest of the poor."

The Missionaries of Charity number some 1500 members throughout the world. In the South Bronx the figure is much more modest: 18 sisters in various stages of training. They minister to a poor quite different from those the order cares for in Asia. In the South Bronx people are not literally dying in the streets for want of food and housing; they are not suffering from leprosy. Nevertheless their needs are as challenging. Most receive assistance or a welfare check of some kind. Still, they barely survive in a vast neighborhood that resembles a bombed-out war zone instead of a corner of a city which is probably the most affluent in the world. As the mission's superior once worded it to the media, in the South Bronx one finds another kind of need, one that is emotional rather than material. As an instance she cited the case of an old woman with two dogs she never allowed out of the apartment. Before the sisters could begin to help her they literally had to shovel the apartment clean.

A young American member of the community was asked what attracted her to the Missionaries of Charity. She replied with a sentence that is testament to everything the sisterhoods stand for historically and currently: "The sincerity of the way of life, striving to live the Gospel message."

The perception of nuns "striving to live the Gospel message" has been a constant, historically, in Roman Catholicism. What was temporarily lost sight of, and what the New Nun brings sharply back into focus is the perception of the nun as a professional woman. In their early days the sisterhoods were the only honorable option open to women who wanted a life other than to marry, produce children, and run a home for husband and offspring. Thus they became avenues of individual freedom and self-expression. Women could teach in schools or nurse in hospitals. They could work with prisoners or the handicapped. They could care for the orphaned. They could travel the world as missionaries. And in these roles they could develop skills generally beyond the attainment of the busy housewife of yesterday. In the early days of Christianity nuns were the first women as a sizable group to learn to read and write, to develop artistic skills, to achieve cultural goals, to become specialists in education as teachers, and in medicine as nurses. Nuns were the female professional class.

Times changed, of course. The "honorable options" open to women became less and less "a husband or a wall," to use Michelle Bernstein's phrase from *The Nuns.* A housewife and mother could develop her intellectual and artistic talents, and she could have a professional life. No less so can nuns. Indeed, nuns as a group are freer to express themselves as persons and to take their place in the world than ever before in history. For the doors to the world are wider than they have ever been. The New Nun is in the world, and the world is glad to have her *back.*

The word back is emphasized because initially this is where she was—in the world. Somewhere along the line the sister got institutionalized and virtually lost behind a convent wall. The founders of her congregation were invariably on the cutting edge of the social issues of their times. But gradually over the years congregation after congregation of sisters withdrew and became almost reclusive. They were in the world, but they were not part of it. The result was something akin to anonymity. Sister's role was defined by someone else, and that someone else was not even of her own gender. Her acquiescence was presumed, and generally she did not disappoint. It was not healthy for the sisterhoods, for sisters individually, nor in some cases for the apostolates that were theirs. More than one congregation that was founded to serve the poor found itself ministering to a fat and satisfied middle class. The condition may have been spawned by the upward mobility of particular classes of people being served by the congregations. Still, the development did drag the congregations away from their apostolic roots.

The New Nun rebels against this. By and large she is anxious to recapture the spirit which brought her congregation into being—and that was the meeting of some urgent social need. Like the early members of her congregation, the New Nun prefers the living of the provisional. She sees security as an inhibitor, a seeming blessing that in fact is enervating of apostolic life. As one sister worded it in terms of her own sisterhood: "The security of convent life is a kind of trap. We fall into it and lose sight of the people and the world where the real needs are."

The New Nun leads a provisional life. She struggles with rent and a food budget. She holds a job. She pays her way (and those who are able contribute something back to the motherhouse). More pertinently, the New Nun is committed to people in their secular situation. People in need: the poor and the powerless.

In the pages following the reader will meet ten such persons. In their own words unfolds the New Nun's commitment, her living of the Corporal and Spiritual Works of Mercy, the Beatitudes—in sum, the Gospel word.

Some of the ideas expressed by the sisters, some of their activities, some of their hopes may strike readers as daring and shocking, but as Sister Mary Loftus, director of information for the Chicago Province of the Sisters of Mercy, said not long ago to *Chicago Tribune* reporter Bruce Buursma, sisters "have always been doing daring and shocking things." Then she uttered a sentence which sums up the church's challenge and the sisters' response: "This is a new age, and it requires new ideas and new dreams."

Part II

Profiles in Commitment

1

Over the Convent Wall for the Seminary

It is a quiet street back of Catholic University—tidy, interracial, unmistakably Washington. The buildings are low-slung, the bricks gleaming red. The street is lined with taxicabs, but the cabs are not there to pick up or discharge passengers. They are home with their drivers. This is no street of diplomats; it is a street of people with more modest occupations, people who grow a few tomatoes out back and cut their own lawn out front. Several obviously drive cabs. Like their drivers, the cabs are resting between rush hours. It is midafternoon.

I ring the bell of a rowhouse and climb to the second floor where I am greeted by a woman in middle years dressed in casual shirt and sweater. Eyes do not have to search out identifying cross or other religious emblem for me to know she is a nun. We have met before, although we are not long friends. I know her 80-year-old mother better than I know her.

She is Mary Irving, a School Sister of Notre Dame, and she opens the door to an apartment that is tastefully but simply decorated—standard divan, easy chairs, some family mementos. Most of the furniture, it will become clear as we talk, was picked up at garage sales. There is a plethora of plants around the place, most sitting on the floor before the broad sun window. Among them, also on the floor, is a crucifix and an open Bible resting on a decorative pillow.

There in her living room Irving could be anyone's average next-door neighbor. Except, of course, she is anything but average. She goes out each morning to work, and she is back home in the evening. But she is not returning from your work-a-day Washington job. Irving is a spiritual director in a men's seminary. That you would never guess along Eighth Street, North East, for Mary Irving has shed the habit and the veil; she dresses as might any woman her age with a job at the Navy Department or at Defense. And as might already be surmised, she has given up her name in religion and gone back to her baptismal name.

Today's nun is engaged in all sorts of new activities, but nothing seems to puzzle old-line Catholics more than this giving up of religious name and religious garb. Even many who are totally receptive to the new roles that so many nuns have assumed for themselves, individually and as a group, have trouble with this business of name and garb. Is it a frivolous action? Is the clothing aspect an act of defiance that daily becomes more glaring in the light of Pope John Paul II's stated preference that women religious dress as women religious historically have?

Irving gets impatient with the questions, and she responds to them only because I insist that in order to know the New Nun at all one must have some understanding of why she shed the habit and reverted to her family name. As she spoke it became clear that practical and, in the instance of name, deep spiritual considerations dictated the decisions.

"I was one of the first persons in my community to experiment with going without a veil," Irving says. "That was back in the late 1960s, early 1970s, right after we changed from the traditional habit. At the time I was in a parish that was more progressive, more forward-looking than most in terms of being inserted into the secular life of the area. I was there, incidentally, as coordinator of religious education. I worked ecumenically, and I began to perceive the veil as a barrier to people, including people in the parish. It did not encourage the kind of lay independence and maturity which I felt we had to be encouraging in parish life."

So Irving and the sister with whom she was working at the time did their little experiment. They surveyed people before and after, and found that in fact many related to them much more freely without the veil. "It seemed to foster a sense of us all working together, rather than my being the boss and everyone having to do what I said," she recalls.

But if Irving was a pioneer on the garb question, she wasn't impulsively so. "I was on our provincial chapter at the time we sisters started having more voice in our lives," she comments, "and I can assure you that we took a long, long time with the habit question. I'd say it was two or three years. Chapter members studied. We had the sisters study. We got experts in to talk to us about the history of the garb. We looked at our own experience as women in the church. We looked at what medieval habits said. We explored the issue of sign value—that is, witness of clothing versus witness of life." The decision reached is all around us in the American church and not just among School Sisters of Notre Dame: A vast number of the sisters do not consider the traditional religious garb as being essential to their lives.

The reversion to baptismal name resulted from an equally conscientious process.

Some theologies of religious life viewed the taking of a new name in religion as akin to the undergoing of a new baptism. There was a validity to that logic, but for people like Irving the practice smacked of elitism, and elitism bothers her. She wanted to honor her own Baptism, and if this desire returned some individuality to her, so much the better.

"I remember being very enthused about Vatican Council II, reading the documents, and coming to a much deeper understanding about the primacy of Baptism in the life of the Christian," she declared. "I also came to see a need for religious people not to separate themselves in a seemingly superior way from the laity—although canonically we are laity too. I began to question accretions that had grown into religious life: the new name, the different garb, the total separation, the withdrawal from the world. All those separation patterns had to be given a second look in the light of the Council. So when we were given the option of keeping our religious name or going back to our baptismal name, I reverted back. I wanted to be known more as a woman of the church, who happens to be a religious. I did not want the religious part to be almost stronger than the church part."

This makes eminent sense. But what if the Pope *orders* sisters back into the habit (he does not seem unduly disturbed by changing of names)? Irving just cannot imagine that happening. She does not even consider the question a worthy concern for a pope. She feels there must be many more important issues awaiting attention on the Pope's desk than how sisters should dress in a modern age and an updated church. It is hard to fault that logic.

The problem for Irving, and some others like her, is that one of those "important issues" may cost her more than a wardrobe; it may cost her the novel job that is hers in the post-Vatican II church.

Mary Irving is a spiritual director in the Paulist father's seminary adjacent to Catholic University. When I was in Washington interviewing her Catholic circles were buzzing with rumors that Pope John Paul II and the Roman Curia were close to a decision that would ban female spiritual directors in male seminaries. The rumor seemed easy enough to credit given the disqualification of women from acting as extraordinary ministers of communion during the papal visit to the United States. Ostensibly the ground on which the decision would be based is that seminarians consulting a spiritual director should be able, if they so desire, to make a sacramental confession to that person. Since women are not empowered to give absolution, this faculty being reserved to priests, then it follows that they cannot act as spiritual directors in seminaries. Simple syllogistic conclusion.

Irving is not losing sleep over the prospect of an edict emanating from Rome separating her from her position. The future will take care of itself. For the meantime there is her work at the seminary, a unique work when one thinks back over the centuries since Trent. Nonclerical spiritual directors, men and women, were once an integral part of church history, but that tradition has been largely lost in the last 300 or 400 years. About ten years ago the tradition was resurrected in the United States, although on a very small scale. Irving is not the first woman spiritual director in an American seminary, but she is in the first wave. She has been in the work for two years, hardly an eye-blink as the church measures time, but a long enough period for one to appreciate the novelty of the situation. "It is a new thing that women should be trained in spiritual direction," she concedes, "and also it is revolutionary that seminaries should recognize the importance of having women on their administrations and their formation teams." The trend pleases her.

Seminarians see many people during their training, for many reasons. They see academic people to help them with their academic lives. They see formation teams to help them examine how they are integrating into the religious community. The focus of Irving's work is to help the seminarians look at their relationship with God. "It centers," she says, "pretty much on their faith life. That would include helping them look at how their prayer life is developing, and how their regular life is developing in terms of Paulist life and academic life. For instance, is there a sense of recognition of the faith dimension and God's presence in it? What hints do the seminarians have of what God is inviting them to? What is happening in their liturgical and prayer life?" In a word she deals with topics touching seminarians' life in common, their theological education, their faith, their experiences. There were 12 seminarians in her charge, so to speak, at the time of our interview.

The obvious question is whether there is any built-in barrier between male seminarian and female spiritual director, and whether there is any danger of the female spiritual director slipping into a kind of mother-figure role in the seminary compound. Irving is quick to dismiss any problem.

There is no "built-in barrier," she says. In fact, she adds, "numbers of seminarians are really glad that there is at least one woman in the formation program to whom they can relate. Many choose me as their spiritual director—or some, anyway—because they want a woman's viewpoint and because they feel that maybe a woman can help them in their spiritual life. There are occasions when some students would rather see a male spiritual director, and that's no problem for me at all. Indeed, if a student is having a man-woman problem or if a student were relating to me so much like his mother that it was interfering with his ministry, then I'd say, 'Let's take a look at this. Maybe you'd rather have someone else. It would be more helpful for your growth.'"

As for the "mother-figure" suggestion, Irving bristles because she does not perceive of herself as a motherly person in the traditional sense, and partly also because the "mother-figure" allusion draws inevitable comparisons to the father figures that so many seminary spiritual directors had a reputation for being in the pre-Vatican II era. Mary Irving has a jaundiced opinion of some of those directors and the system under which they worked. "Before the Council, most of the spiritual directors' emphasis would have been on the externals, juridical requirements of the faith," she explains. "Were the individuals attending the sacraments regularly? Were they praying? There was probably less attention paid to the quality of one's relationship with God. In talking with priests I find a cross section of attitudes towards the old spiritual directors. Some priests don't want to be reminded of them. They were not strong, positive father figures. They were 'requirements' of a sort that you had to put up with. I don't want to be that kind of spiritual director, so I don't think of myself as a counterpart mother figure. And I don't want the students to perceive me as a mother figure. I prefer that they think of me as a friend. Or companion."

Inevitably one must wonder how long a woman spiritual director for seminarians would be satisfied in that role. It has to be terribly frustrating to help move persons to ordination, knowing at the same time that ordination is barred to you because of your gender. Would Irving take Holy Orders if the sacrament were available to her?

She finds that a hard question. The answer she advances deals less with the seminarians with whom she is working, surprisingly, than with the retreat work which engages her in the summertime. When we talked she was looking ahead to a week-long retreat for married people that she would be assisting a priest with up on Cape Cod. "I feel that I am really called to celebrate Eucharist," she said, "and I feel it especially not only since I have gotten into spiritual direction, but also retreat work. It's only natural that when you're with a group of women or men for a retreat, for a week or a weekend, that you should be able to celebrate the Eucharist with them. Or the Sacrament of Reconciliation. It's a natural outflow of the ministry. So yes, in a sense I feel a calling to the priesthood. It's new to me. It hasn't been fully tested. It can't be. But I would say I feel a call."

Then she added a codicil that I was to encounter time and again in my conversations with nuns for this book: She does not feel a call to the priesthood as it exists today in a clerical structure. Others were more explicit than she on the subject, but she made it apparent she was referring to the institutionalism that attends the modern priesthood: rectory life, the set patterns of ministry on the diocesan level, the system of preferments and promotions. The trappings of ministry, in sum, leave her in the middle on the ordination issue.

Sister Mary Irving is a native of Boston. She was born in 1934 and entered the School Sisters of Notre Dame in 1952, when she was 18 years old. She received her bachelor of arts degree from the College of Notre Dame of Maryland, a masters in French from Assumption College in Worcester; then in the 1970s, when so many sisters were returning to school for special training to equip them to function in a wider role in an updated church, she attended the Weston School of Theology in Cambridge, Mass. There she received a master of theology degree in spiritual direction.

Inevitably a decision to change the course of one's lifework in middle years raises questions. The change of emphasis in Irving's took her from teacher in parochial schools to spiritual director in a seminary, with an intermediate step as coordinator of religious education at a parish in Columbia, Md. She entered religious life obviously to be a school teacher; indeed that vocational objective is in the name of her order. And she was a school teacher—for five years on the elementary level in Baltimore, and for eight years on the high-school level in Towson, Md. How does someone like Irving look back on a life that in effect has been jettisoned? Does she miss those years? Does she feel they have been wasted?

Irving's response is tinged with the bittersweet found so commonly among Catholics who grew up in the pre-Vatican II church.

"I have a sense of having moved from one world to another," she says. "My old world was much more the Catholic ghetto. It was the 1950s. There were set systems. If you wanted to dedicate your life to God, you became a sister. And sisters taught. So most likely you joined the order you had in high school, and you did what they told you to do. That usually meant teaching. Now within those structures there were many good things happening—growing experiences, learning experiences. Many people in my religious community are still in teaching, and they find it a positive experience for them professionally and as a ministry. But that life is light years away from me now."

Irving comments that when she began training for spiritual direction, she discovered a side of her that she never knew existed. While she loved teaching, she says, she felt far more comfortable with spiritual direction. "It gave me a whole different perspective," she explains. "I had been a good and effective teacher. I had been happy in the work for 13 years. And maybe—who knows?—I would have stayed with it for the rest of my life. But new things started happening in the 1960s and 1970s, and I got attracted to a whole new way of working in the church. It was like finding a new home."

It is a story with which I was to become very familiar in talking to New Nuns—a story of not looking back with regrets, but of looking back from quite a distance; a story of being glad for the years as a young religious, years generally spent in teaching, but of being happier to be working now at "other things."

Of course a decision to go on to "other things" leaves those who remain with the old apostolate in the lurch, as it were. Father Richard McBrien, the theologian and writer, once wrote in his syndicated diocesan newspaper column of the bitterness that exists in some nuns, particularly older nuns, who have devoted a lifetime to teaching in parochial schools, and who, with the replacement in Catholic consciousness of the importance of parochial schools, and the gravitation of younger sisters to "other things," feel not only abandoned but also as if they have wasted their lives and careers. Do people like Irving aggravate psychological feelings such as those?

"I've had to take a hard look at that objection," she admits. "I'm sympathetic, but I don't agree with it. I've tried hard to convince people that it isn't necessarily disbelief in the parochial school system to leave it for something new. But many older sisters—and some young ones, too—are quite rigidly tied into the Catholic school system. They're tied in a way I could never be in the church today—not after having seen so much broadening of the church. The needs of the church are too many for me to take the Catholic school and make it my first priority."

There is a tone of independence in the comment, but not of arrogance or callousness. "We keep doors open with each other," she declares. "We try to do things to let each other know the experiences of other ministries. For instance we have apostolate days where we seek to learn about each other." But she concedes that feelings of bitterness, and perhaps betrayal, are not going to disappear overnight—"at least not in my community, which includes the word school in its very name."

A point to be marked about the New Nun is that she is anything but a one-dimensional person, moving in the main between office and residence, much as she moved previously between classroom and convent. She is very much a person of the world, deeply involved in national and international issues of social and political character. And, because she refuses to be a second-class member of the church, she is deeply involved too in ecclesiastical issues on which she would one day never have raised a voice. Not on a dare. Irving is such a person, and she speaks for her kind.

"The whole area of social consciousness opened up for sisters about the same time, roughly, that religious life did after the Council," she states. "Significant numbers of sisters read the Council documents, notably the Church in the Modern World, and took them seriously in terms of developing an openness to the world which we never had before. The documents were really revolutionary for me, because I had accepted the theology that the whole point of religious life was to cut you off from the world. You were to pray for it, but its concerns were not yours. All that has changed."

Irving notes the development of her own thinking and confesses, with what seems wonder and excitement, that she does not know when or where the process will end. "I find myself responding to the El Salvador issues"—by

which she means the political oppression there that de-
humanizes the people and persecutes church workers,
such as the four women missionaries, three of them nuns,
who were murdered in December, 1980. "I find myself
responding to the Reagan administration's budget cuts,"
she continues. "My life is much more open to political
realities than ever it was, and I sense myself becoming
more determined to make my voter's voice known." She
has also placed her body on the line. She pickets nuclear-
arms bazaars; she has been arrested and convicted for
praying on the White House lawn in protest over budget
cuts for the poor, over the arms race, and, again, El Salvador policy. "I see myself at the beginning of a journey,"
she says. "I don't know where it's going to lead ultimately,
but I certainly see myself moving more directly in concern
for public issues."

And church issues, too, for like New Nuns as a whole
Irving considers herself a second-class member of the
church—not in terms of the mind of Jesus and what she
regards as his intention for men and women in the church,
but rather in terms of the structure of the church. "I am
convinced I'm of equal dignity to anybody else," she says
with feeling. "But from what has happened structurally,
and I'm thinking specifically of Holy Orders, there's no
doubt in my mind that women are second-class members
of the church." And it is not the ordination issue alone that
makes her feel that way. It is the decision-making procedure, which she thinks exists almost as a way of Catholicism. "We are a hierarchical church, and the life of the
church is determined in major part by the clerics of the
church. That's a problem that extends outward. It is separate from the whole problem of lay participation in the

church. From the point of view of women, it comes down to this: As long as those belonging to one half of the human race make the decisions and set the rules for the whole membership, you have a disorder."

She returns to the issue of garb: "The people who raised the issue and will make the decision have absolutely no experience of the life of women. It doesn't make sense that the group with the responsibility of making the decision has nobody on it who has any real experience. It cuts out half the church's membership from the possibility of having a voice in decisions that affect their lives. The church is male in the power it has taken to itself, and that's a tremendous loss for the church. Women aren't heard. That's fundamental in our experience. The longer the situation goes on, the harder it's going to be for us to be heard. There's a parallel in the 1980 Synod on the Christian family. The bishops talked about marriage, and there were just a few married people there. It's so distorted, it's humorous—except peoples' lives are affected by it."

But the issue that agitates her most is that of the exclusion of women from ordination—this, despite the fact that she is not certain she would even take Holy Orders in its present clerical construct. Thus it was that Irving was one of the 53 sisters who stood in silent protest to the "deafness" of Pope John Paul II on women during his 1979 address at the National Shrine of the Immaculate Conception in Washington. She tells of a planning meeting held beforehand at which the women were asked to declare why they were there and why they were willing to stand in protest. Irving found herself saying that women's language isn't listened to in the church, and that they had to move to bodily language of gesture in order to penetrate the deafness of the church to women.

The day the sisters stood was of course the famous day that Sister M. Theresa Kane, then president of the Leadership Conference of Women Religious, delivered the greeting to the Pope in which she called on the church to demonstrate concern for human dignity by "providing the possibility of women as persons being included in all ministries of our church." To some it appeared to be a pincer attack—Kane hitting from one side and the 53 sisters from another. But there was nothing co-ordinated in the actions; you can take it from Mary Irving. "Theresa Kane did not know that we sisters were going to stand, and we sisters did not know that she was going to say what she did," she says. "The two came together and looked planned, but they weren't. It was just a strange coincidence."

Television cameras zoomed in, it will be remembered, on the standing sisters, and the face of Sister Mary Irving, S.S.N.D., flashed from Washington to Hawaii to points around the world. She was an instant celebrity—and controversialist. Most of the mail she received from those who recognized her was positive. But there was negative reaction within her religious community.

"Maybe five or six sisters of my province stood," Irving recalls, "and a large group of sisters wrote our provincial and said they thought this was very disrespectful of the Holy Father." Objections centered also on garb. The Pope had just come from Philadelphia, where he had said that he wanted sisters to wear the habit, and here the next day in Washington were several School Sisters of Notre Dame not only standing in what seemed impolite and disloyal fashion, but also defiantly out of garb. In an attempt to sooth troubled waters, Irving and others of her 53 colleagues went to provincial headquarters in Baltimore and had a three-hour conference/dialogue with those who objected. "We wanted to try to help them understand where we were coming from," Irving says, "and we in turn wanted to understand their feelings and reactions." The results were mixed. The standees did not persuade the objectors as a group, but Irving is convinced that they all came away understanding one another better.

For her own part in the Washington protest she has never had a minute of regret. She believes the gesture of the 53 was of historic importance, for the figurative statement it made that American women religious take themselves seriously, and for the evidence it conveyed that they will look for creative ways to call attention to situations in the church that cry for correction. "For me," says Mary Irving, "it boils down to a conflict between the *refined* sister-woman, who would never be impolite to a guest, and an *honest* sister-woman, who would say this is an issue of justice and dignity. Honesty far outweighed an apparent lack of politeness to a guest. That was at the heart of my decision to stand."

Would she do it again?

"I definitely would," she answers.

2

From Stamford to the End of the Road

One has to know Stamford, Conn. to begin to understand a decision to exchange life there for St. Charles, Va.
Stamford is exurban New York—affluent, roomy, secure,
a city new-born as a corporate headquarters center, a city
with a future which almost certainly will be grander than
its past. St. Charles? Well, as a Glenmary priest once commented to Sister Beth Davies, C.N.D., "It is the end of the
road."

Christ stopped at Eboli; he never got near St. Charles.
St. Charles is a coal-mining town deep in the Appalachian
Mountains. It is Appalachia in spades—poor, struggling,
remote. If its future proves better than its past, it will be
because its past has been so gloomy that any future is
bound to be brighter. In the 1930s St. Charles was at least
a busy little place. But that was when coal was king. When
oil took over as the primary heating fuel in the late 1940s
and early 1950s, a number of coal camps shut down, and
thousands of miners and their families moved on—to Cin-
cinnati, Chicago, Philadelphia, Dayton. Those who stayed
behind were mostly people without alternatives. They
hunkered down in and around St. Charles, people without

prospects or resources, ghostly figures in a ghost-like town. Even today there are only 368 people within the corporate limits of St. Charles, and 2500 within the post office area. Most live in isolated pockets of the mountain.

And Sister Beth Davies—former grade-school teacher on Manhattan's Lower West Side; former high-school teacher, then principal in Connecticut—went to them. It is an interesting story.

In the early 1970s Davies was principal of Stamford Catholic High School, and a feature of the curriculum was a program for seniors in the last six months of their training. The program included work experiences and seminars that sought to raise the social consciousness of students to the world around them. One such was a Christian Humanism seminar conducted by a Maryknoll priest and a Glenmary brother. Three quarters of the way through, the students were encouraged to have a direct experience with life in an area of rural poverty—a species all its own from the urban poverty the student might see in Stamford or nearby New York City. The Glenmary priests and brothers work in the Appalachian Mountains, and through them the school set up a couple of weeks' experience in the Appalachian region. "The response was marvelous," Davies remarks. "Parents came to me to talk about the impact of the experience on their children. Some students wanted to return to the area as volunteers during the summer. We even had graduates who completed college and returned to full-time work in the area."

But Davies had not gone to Appalachia herself, and in time that began to gnaw at her: "I wanted to spend some time in the area and get a feel of what it was that attracted so many to want to go back. I wanted to be more knowledgeable when speaking to parents." So in the summer of 1971 she arranged through Glenmary to spend two weeks in Appalachia, visiting in Virginia, North Carolina, Tennessee, and Kentucky. It was a momentous trip, and it changed the whole course of Davies's life as a woman religious.

She went to Appalachia that first time with a sister-companion, and they spoke with many people to get a sense of the economic conditions of the area. "The thing that struck me most," she recalls, "was the very rich land and very poor people. I had a lot of questions, because little seemed to make sense. I heard people talk about their terribly bitter winters and their inability to heat their homes, and these same homes were sitting on coal. I couldn't figure this out." Nor could she figure the religious situation. She came from a part of the world where the parishes were laid out in city blocks, organized and efficient, and well staffed. Here it was different. "I particularly remember one area in southwest Virginia," she comments. "A Glenmary priest drove me around, and we went for miles and miles and miles. He had a couple of counties to cover, and those counties were his parish. One county alone was 440-square miles. He kept saying, 'This is my parish, and this is my parish, and I've never been here, and I've never been here.' He was the only Catholic minister in the area. There wasn't another priest, sister, brother, or lay minister. He was the only one. My eyes were opened. I was appalled."

It did not take Davies long to come to her decision. On

the drive back to Connecticut, she turned to her companion and said, "Louise, I'm going back there." Louise said, "You're crazy." Davies said, "I'm going back."

It all sounds very impulsive, but there was more working beneath the surface. Beth Davies had been a member of the Congregation of Notre Dame since 1953, entering when she was 20. She held bachelor's and master's degrees from Fordham and Columbia, and had a Sixth Year Degree in educational administration as well, also from Columbia. Her past, her present, and presumably her future were to be in education. But fate decreed differently. "I knew for probably three years that the Scriptures were speaking to me very differently," Davies says. "Everyday I was hearing the Word in a new way. The challenge deepened. I knew that someday, somehow, I wanted to be identified with the poor in some way. I felt the Lord was leading me to that. I didn't know where, and I didn't know what it would be. But as soon as I was in the mountains, something clicked."

And so the process began. There was a year remaining on her contract with the Diocese of Bridgeport—Stamford Catholic High being a diocesan school—and she would fulfill that. She would also have to convince her religious congregation that the mission she contemplated was within the vocational sphere of the order, and this went smoothly. ("The only stipulations were that our mission had to be a community of three, as we were going into a very isolated area, and that we would have to be self-supporting, because the order could not completely subsidize many such missions. It was expected too that we have the opportunity for frequent liturgies.") There followed the formation of the team, and a sister from Illinois and another from Canada responded to a blind "call" to join a mission to Appalachia. Finally there was the selection of location. The last proved the knottiest of the details, and its working-out testified to the seriousness of purpose of Beth Davies.

She went back to Appalachia in February; this was now 1972. With her were the two others who would form their mission of three. It was important, thought Davies, for the three of them to "feel" as a team the isolation of the place. "We were all urban people," she remarks, "and the area offered none of the activities taken for granted in the city." In addition they had to decide exactly where they would sink roots.

They inquired of a Glenmary priest, "Where is the place where people seem to be most down and out?" He said St. Charles. He did not know it well; he had been there maybe one or two times at most, but from what he observed, and from what people said repeatedly, St. Charles was it. "It is the end of the road."

The three called on the man who headed the Office of Economic Opportunity in the area back in the War on Poverty days, and they asked his advice. "We talked a bit," Davies says, "and he asked, 'Why are you coming here?' I said, 'I really can't answer that.' And he said, 'What are you going to do?' I said, 'Well, I don't know what we're going to do. We won't know until we're here. We've got to listen.' And he said edgily, 'You're not coming with any hard objectives?' I said, 'No, we're coming to listen.' Then he changed. He softened, and he said, 'Well, if you want to know the area that I would suggest, if you want the worst area in this part of Virginia, it's St. Charles.'" Of course it was the very place mentioned by the Glenmary priest.

But the former OEO official was not finished talking. He added, "If one family—no, if one person has a little more hope because you've been there, it's worth all your effort." That spoke volumes to Beth Davies. "Here we are," she says, "turning out hundreds of graduates a year and producing this and that, and here he's saying that if just one person has a little more hope because you've been there, it's worth all the effort. That's Gospel language."

So the little band of sisters from the Congregation of Notre Dame settled on St. Charles. Settling in was somewhat more complicated. "First of all, we were Yankees; second, we were Catholics; third, we were sisters"—that is the way Davies sums up the ingredients of the "welcome." That made housing difficult to procure. Walls would go up when landlords learned who was seeking the rental. That made community acceptance considerably less than automatic. In fact during the first few years in town the local Baptist minister censured them Sunday after Sunday from the pulpit. The great fear seemed to be that the sisters were there to snatch up people for the Catholic Church—"not an unfounded fear," as Davies admits. But of course they were not there to convert people. They were there to listen—and to help. As this became clear, hostility melted away (although not all), and even the Baptist minister was lauding "those three sister-women" from his pulpit.

The breakthrough came in small but meaningful ways: through volunteer work at the community center, where people would come to learn arts and crafts, or to learn to read and write (one of the sisters prepares people for the grade-equivalency diploma); through the arranging of a health fair in conjunction with Vanderbilt University Medical School (most of the people of St. Charles had never had a full physical); through what might be typed the modern corporal works of mercy—assisting old people through the Social Security process; guiding the poor who might not know they were eligible for welfare payments or food stamps; protecting the work benefits and insurance rights of miners.

Davies tells of an incident that occurred shortly after she had arrived in the region. A strip miner came off the mountain on a bulldozer and smashed his arm. The man, named Elmer, was taken to the hospital, and he was no sooner there than his wife called Beth Davies saying the mine operator was at the hospital and he wanted Elmer to sign a paper. Elmer does not read or write, and neither does the wife. Davies told her, "Don't sign anything. Ask him to leave the paper there. I'll come over and we'll go over it together, then if Elmer wants to sign it, fine." Needless to say, when she got to the hospital there was no paper. "The operator wanted Elmer to sign away all company liability for the accident," she believes.

As a result of her becoming seriously involved in that case Davies experienced the first threat on her life. Subsequently there were others. (A mine security officer once pulled a gun when she was showing a foreign journalist over a stripped landscape.) She chooses not to dwell on incidents such as these. "Greed makes people violent," she will merely say. "I had never experienced it so closely before. There's no need to go into detail about some of the threats. When we 'stand with the least in the struggle for justice,' there's a price to pay."

For the first year in St. Charles Davies considered herself nothing but a listening presence. Her objective was to get to know and to hear from people. Gradually she worked into the community.

"I worked a great deal in the beginning with men who should have been getting black-lung benefits," she recounts, "people who had applied for benefits years before and were not receiving them. Or others who had never applied because they didn't know what to do with the papers. They couldn't read them, and they didn't want to admit that they couldn't. Too many of them were giving that work to lawyers, and the lawyers were taking a large cut in the benefits. And there was no work to it at all. If one could read and write, one didn't need any legal background to get black-lung benefits for families. There are lawyers in eastern Kentucky who have become millionaires almost overnight on the money they received from black-lung cases."

In time big things began to happen in St. Charles. A health council was organized as a direct result of the health fair, and out of it came St. Charles' own clinic. St. Charles now has a doctor from the National Health Service Corps, which is a federally funded program for medically impoverished areas. It also has a nurse practitioner. The clinic's equipment and a pharmacy came by way of grants of $30,000 and $14,000, respectively, from the U.S. Bishops' Campaign for Human Development, that meritorious program which raises funds for social and humanitarian projects which would otherwise be beyond institutional reach. After the success of the health clinic, the community became more confident in its ability to effect change and formed its own chapter of Virginia Citizens for Better Reclamation, a local citizens' group organized to stop irresponsible strip mining—strip mining of the sort that has left the area permanently scarred ("We call it the rape of the mountains," says Davies) and which has opened towns like St. Charles to a constant threat of flooding. (The town has experienced several floods since Beth Davies's arrival.) Finally, at the time of my interviewing, an alcoholism treatment center was in the making for the area.

The obvious question in looking into the life of a person like Sister Beth Davies, C.N.D. is to ask whether she is a mere community organizer—a good community organizer, to be sure, but more community organizer than she is woman religious. After all, it is as woman religious that she is defined both in vocational calling and in the very way that she signs her name.

Davies rejects the notion. She is convinced that the call of the church today is to work with the poor, whereas as teacher and principal she was identifying with the middle and upper-middle class—the class into which yesterday's poor had evolved. She is convinced that she is both where God wants her and where she is needed most. And most emphatically she is convinced that she is not wasting her time or her talent.

"Some people say to me, 'What are you doing? You're not using your background, your talent. Why are you wasting your time?' That saddens me. Never have I been richer or happier."

On the other side of the coin, she rejects the notion that she is hero and inspiration. "The poor of St. Charles should be interviewed today," she says. "*They* are the inspiration. I have learned that *we* need the poor much more than the poor need us. I firmly believe that we need to go to the poor to be evangelized. I think it is only through such struggle and pain, such *powerlessness,* that people realize their need for God. The poor understand so well what total dependence on God means. In Appalachia I have gained more than I have given. There's no doubt about it. I'm not just saying that. Working among the poor has taught me something about my God and about my vocation that all the theology, all the training never taught me. Maybe it's because one doesn't have to cut through a facade. Their simplicity is profound. It's just so easy to find the presence of God among his poor. One doesn't have to search. He's there. God *is* simple. I've been privileged."

Further, Davies would deny that her life is in fact so totally divorced from institutional concerns. For instance she was involved in the evolution of the 1975 pastoral letter, "This Land Is Home to Me," which was issued by the bishops of the 13 states of Appalachia. For a year and a half she was part of the team that gathered the data on which the pastoral was based. The team talked with people working on social issues. They went in the "hollers" and did tape after tape with people who historically never had a thing to say about what was happening to them. They talked of their lives, their struggles, their hopes—and if all the data did not go into the writing, it went into the background for the written document. "There probably was never a more documented pastoral than that one," remarks Davies. "We had everything on tapes. We had it in writing. This magnificent document was truly a response to the cries of Appalachia's poor."

Inevitably it must be asked how a Catholic maintains a sacramental life in a town, which has only one full-time church, and it is Baptist, and but two small missionary churches, neither of which is Catholic. If nothing more, it would seem a challenge to fulfill her religious congregation's admonition to attend frequent liturgies.

Where worship is concerned, Davies feels neither deprived nor particularly inconvenienced. She and her colleagues generally worship in a mission church maintained about 10 miles from St. Charles by the central parish in Big Stone Gap. It is just a little house, but it is "delightful," to use Davies's word. Just a handful of people worship at that church. They come from that 440-square-mile area, some traveling an hour or more to get there. "It is a very small community, a very beautiful community," Davies says—although there are uncomfortable moments. "You see, many of the Catholics in the Appalachian region are transplants from urban areas," she explains. "Mostly they're management people with the coal companies, and unfortunately they're often people who are standing on the other side of issues. This makes it awkward. We go to church with people from management, but we're standing with people in contention with management. It does make for conflict at times."

Davies actually finds worshiping in Appalachia stimulating and inspiring. "Ministry there is just very different," she says. "It's just understood that sometimes the priest cannot be present. If the priest cannot get there for Sunday Mass, well then the community takes over." There will be readings, a homily, and then a communion service, a lay minister distributing hosts from a eucharistic reserve maintained for such a circumstance.

At moments like this does the worshiping community look to Davies to take the leadership in religious services, leading the prayers, directing the service, distributing communion? It doesn't, because when she went to Appalachia she was adamant about not being identified as an institutional person, belonging to a cadre. She was also firm about not being hired by a diocese or parish, on the theory that where the money is, there the power is. "If I were going to be paid by either a diocese or a parish," she comments, "then they could determine—and reasonably so—what I should or should not do." So she maintains an arm's length, even at priestless Sunday services.

"You take a map of the county we live in, this 440-square-miles with 25,000 people," she comments. "You take a little dot. That's the number of Catholics in it: 25 people out of 25,000. Well, we didn't choose to move into that area to minister to just a little dot. We chose to be in that area to identify with the poorest, and they are not in the Catholic tradition."

It's not surprising, therefore, that she is not one who craves Holy Orders. She believes in ordination for women; she is a strong advocate that male and female, both, are called to ordination; she is persuaded that one day there will be ordained female and male, married and unmarried—and that "people of tomorrow who read our history will chuckle at all the fuss." But ordination is not for her. She has no desire for it, never has, and most certainly would never take it in the church "as it is structured today." Once again, that qualifier one hears so often from the New Nun. What does Davies mean by it? "I just see how limited priests are," she answers. "There is very little room for creative ministry. And it is very difficult to be 'servant' when one belongs to the privileged caste. Unfortunately Holy Orders does that—sets people *apart* rather than making them *a part.*"

As far as the institutional church is concerned, if she could change one thing tomorrow it would be to provide for the return to the active ministry of priests who have married. "They're all over this region," she declares, "and they can't minister, at least not in the Catholic Church. And they're doing such magnificent work—ministering, as they say, more than they were ever able to when they were in the formal priesthood. They're very involved in the parishes, and they're real leaders in some parishes. I should add that women have great leadership too in the parishes. There isn't any feeling of male versus female. Whoever shows the leadership is the person who is accepted in that capacity."

When I talked with Davies she was completing studies towards certification as an alcoholism counselor at the Rutgers School of Alcohol Studies, and working as an intern at the Trenton Detox, a social-setting facility which serves that city's indigent population. Certification would represent intellectual accomplishment and provide Davies with an important credential in combating a widespread problem in the mountains. No less important, it would be another milestone in her own overcoming of the disease of alcoholism.

There is a lot of alcoholism in the St. Charles area, Davies remarks—not other drugs so much, as they run into too much money. But alcohol is readily available, and is relatively cheap. Large numbers of people abuse it, and the problem cases get little sympathy and less treatment.

"Too many doors close when you're trying to get people into treatment," says Davies. "The first question asked is, 'Do they have insurance?' 'No.' So the doors are closed so far as they're concerned."

61

On the level of sympathy it is not much better. "Ours, of course, is the Baptist belt," she explains. "It's strongly fundamentalist. It's a sin to drink at all. That's been impressed on people so much that those who drink are just despairing. In trying to encourage people back to health through a better understanding of the disease, one usually hears, 'I'm lost anyway.' Even the doctors in the area need a lot of education. They'll tell patients, 'You've just got to get back to church.' They'll tell parents, 'You've just got to know where your children are all the time.' Then the problem's supposed to go away. It's as though alcoholism doesn't exist."

But no one knows better than Davies that it does exist—and that is why she left the mountains for a year and went to inner-city Trenton for her special training. "I'm here for my own education," she said in her office in a converted motel that was long removed from its glory days. "And I'm here because I'm an alcoholic myself."

She talks with the matter-of-factness of a clinician: "I know a lot about the disease from personal experience, and I know the excellent treatment I was given. The poor deserve no less. It has been a real gift in my life to experience such powerlessness. Through it I am able to identify with the 'oppressed of the oppressed' in the mountains, who are cast aside as moral lepers. Through it I have come to know what it means to die in order to live. That's a gift. Gifts are given not to be kept for oneself; they're given to be shared. I want to share what I have learned, and whom I have come to be, with people who share the same disease."

And so the objective of an alcoholism treatment center. Davies serves on the board of directors of a small hospital in Pennington Gap, not far from St. Charles, and the hospital is in the process of building a new facility. Davies's dream is to get a "detox"—detoxification center—in the hospital. She has been encouraging the board and the administration towards that end. She is also lining up prospective personnel and has found a doctor and a pharmacist who are open-minded on the problem and willing to work in the field. "There are many different people who are dreaming together," says Beth Davies of the project. "So we see ours as not just a dream, but a dream that will become the reality of our own treatment center in the mountains, where the poor will be welcome." It is a challenge, she admits, but she is convinced it can be done— "with God's help."

"We need only trust."

3

Reaching Across Barriers to Other Women

She greets you at the door radiating the warmth and pleasantness of a Washington hostess. Except, of course, she is no hostess and she's running no tea party. She's a Sister of St. Joseph, neat and trim in a green pants ensemble. Her face you know from your own ethnic background. She could be the girl next door whom you knew growing up, and you say to yourself she is aging a lot more gracefully than you are. You wonder at this, for this sister isn't your standard-brand religious, serenely settled in middle life into vocation and assignment. She lives a life of daily challenge in a no-nonsense area of human activity.

This is a woman who, after 25 years of doing the things Sisters of St. Joseph traditionally do, decided that her vocation as sister went in a different direction, one that was strongly and essentially feminist. She broke with diocesan bureaucracy to found a home for battered women, and today she puts in regular hours as a volunteer at that home, while running an adjacent center for reflective action on issues concerning women and peace. She lives the other side of the clock by and large. When most people are heading home from work, her day is often just beginning.

She seems to be thriving under a regimen that would bend others. She is Annette Rafferty, S.S.J.

Night after night she is there at the door of Abby's House on Crown Street in a worn-down section of Worcester, Mass., helping to provide the bottom-line needs, the hospitality, the caring for homeless women and their children, the battered wife, the wandering mentally ill woman, the alcoholic woman presently not drinking, whose Social Security or pension check has been stolen, or who has just mismanaged her money. Abby's House is a place where any woman can come for any reason and have very few questions asked. It is open to whatever the needs are, although some needs are greater than Abby's House's ability to handle them, such as those of the woman who is obviously on drugs, or the woman who is totally drunk and unable to manage with others in the shelter. Abby's House has no "detox" facilities, so it has banded with public programs and crisis centers, whose personnel will come in a van and carry the person to facilities equipped to cope with her condition.

All this begins late in the afternoon and goes on until the doorbell stops ringing or until Abby's House is full. "We can comfortably accommodate 11 women," says Rafferty, "but we've had as many as 17. That would include a woman with maybe nine kids. We push the beds together or put a mattress on the floor. We've never been more than that 17. Most of the time we run four or five a night."

In the daytime hours she is to be found on the other side of the divided old residence, in the peace and justice center called the Worcester Connection, with its emphasis on women's concerns. The Worcester Connection grew out of Abby's House and conclusions reached by Rafferty and her colleagues on the night mission about the "systematic connections between women's economic plight, their homelessness, their inability to afford anything, and some deeper issues of sexism, racism, classism, and, not the least, militarism." The words are Rafferty's. "Here we put energies into a study and educational program for the broader community into the things that cause people to be poor. This side of the house is an independent operation from the shelter, but philosophically it is connected to it because we're still working over here on women's agenda. We have a chapel here rather than in Abby's House because we want to make the justice and peace center open to women and men who have common concerns—to people who would just like to get away from the mad rush of the city, their homes, and come and pray for a day, or come and relax here in this chapel or this room."

For Annette Rafferty all this is a radical departure from the sedate sisterly life that was hers from the time she entered the Sisters of St. Joseph in 1952 at the age of 22, until the 1970s, when she found herself being tugged in new emotional and apostolic ways. For 16 years—from 1955 to 1971—she taught on the high-school level in Holyoke, Newport, Springfield, and Worcester, and from 1971 to 1979 she served on the executive council of her religious community. She had loved teaching, and she looks back on those years with the pleasantest of memories. She emphasized that she did not leave teaching because she was unhappy. She left because she was elected to a leadership position in the order, which happened also to be a full-time job. The job almost suffocated her. But in her distress was her apostolic rebirth.

"I served as what they call an area director for sisters in the Dioceses of Worcester and Providence," Rafferty recalls. "Basically all that was was listening and enabling—helping women to feel comfortable with their own decisions. Remember, for eons we never made any decisions. Then all of a sudden we get into the new chapters of Vatican II and find out that people now can sense their own gifts, and go the way they think the Holy Spirit is calling. It was incredible how many people had to struggle within themselves to resign from a job and move on to something else."

Rafferty says she listened "morning, noon, and night" to people so that they could find their own answers to what they wanted to do in the new church. "I was listening to sisters for over a year," she remarks, "and I thought to myself, 'My God, I don't want to lose a sense of my own ministry. When I'm out of this job I want to know where I'm going with my life.'" She turned to a priest-friend, Father Frank Scollen who was an official of the Worcester diocesan Urban Ministry Commission, and said, "Look, I'm out of active teaching. I'm in a one-to-one with sisters, and I'm almost drowning in a sister world. I want to know how the city works, what needs to be done." In retrospect she says she was really groping for answers to the questions: Are sisterhoods going to be a valid concept for the future? Are there things that only women living in a lifestyle like that of sisters can do? And again, what needs to be done? Father Scollen invited her to join the board of the Urban Ministry—and a whole new world opened up.

The commission set up a task force on homeless women, and Frank Scollen said to Rafferty, "Hey, run with it; it's your baby." She did. She found obvious inspiration in the Jesus of the Gospels, and was to write later in the *Catholic*

Free Press, the Worcester diocesan newspaper, "Just as Jesus was perfectly clear about his priorities, choosing to be with the dispossessed, and alienated, so his life gives women, living a vowed life in community, no other option than 'to do mercy' through their efforts to reach across the barriers that separate them from other women." Spare time from duties on the order's executive council and one whole summer were spent talking to women on the street, asking questions like: Do you have a place to stay? Where do you go when your money runs out and you're really hard up? Is there a place for you? She began to worry that for so many women in the City of Worcester the alternatives were either prostituting outside a seedy downtown hotel, sleeping in the weeds or under bushes, or camping in what was a veritable jungle near a local sweater outlet. She was appalled.

"Between the time I joined the commission and the time I quit, I had done a flip," she remarks. "I had become morally involved in what I was finding."

Thus it was that instead of merely presenting cool data each week at the Urban Ministry meeting, she was presenting hot data with growing anger and a quickening sense that the commission needed to act. But to her the commission seemed to be dragging its feet, so one evening in 1975 she made her announcement. "Look," she said, "we're not going to do anything with this data. I appreciate being here, but I'm going to leave and put my full energies into a coalition to get something started. My decision is irreversible." She recalls that some of the men on the commission got upset with her, and some thought her foolhardy. In effect, what could she, a lone woman religious, do without the diocese's resources?

Rafferty routed the skepticism soon enough. She called

a meeting of the women she had talked to on the street—the solicitors, the down-and-outers, the women who were drunk when she had last met them, and had maybe sobered up. Seventy-five of them drew together, and out of that 75 came a planning committee that continued to meet for three or four months until they had designed a project. They decided on a shelter that would be open every night, all night long, and close at some point in the morning until late in the afternoon of the same day, when it would re-open again. Apart from accenting the emergency dimension of the shelter, the schedule would enable volunteers, on whom it was proposed the shelter depend for staffing, to get to their jobs in the daytime hours.

Meanwhile Rafferty had begun giving little talks to women's groups, stressing the need for a shelter and asking people to contribute to a dream. A women's student organization at Holy Cross College came up with $68.17, thus inaugurating the fund. Months of scratching brought the fund up to $500. Then Rafferty heard that there was $1000 available from the city—available in this sense: A gift had been made to the city manager, Francis McGrath, and he was uncertain how to dispense it. Women members of the City Council encouraged Rafferty to go and ask for it. So she stood in the docket at a City Council meeting. She came up as bill number 16, as she recalls, between two street-light propositions, and she asked if the $1000 might be hers in order that she might open a shelter for homeless women. The questions were only a few, but they were astonishing—or at least one was. "Don't we have one in the city already?" a councilor asked. Rafferty said no. The $1000 was hers. With the $500 already on hand, the shelter was in business in rented quarters on Crown Street. Later they were able to buy the structure.

"Once we opened our doors and people heard about us, it was incredible the way donations came in," says Rafferty. "The Human Development Campaign of the U.S. Catholic Conference gave us a $3000 grant, and my own congregation has been extremely generous with two $3500 grants. Still, we run the shelter mostly on donations and the volunteer stream of women, who have rallied around this issue and have given their time seven nights a week for five years now. Two women a night. That's really a fantastic record."

In due course officials of the state Department of Mental Health visited Abby's House, and left so impressed with the work being done there, particularly in terms of mentally ill women who were being accommodated with shelter, that they arranged part-time salaries for four workers—Sister Elaine Lamoureux, S.S.A., Rafferty's nun-colleague, and three women who themselves were in truly hardship situations. "So it's been an enabling process to have that money coming in here," comments Rafferty. "We've used it to employ women who need money, who needed to be employed."

For its drop-ins the shelter provides a light breakfast and a light supper, although at suppertime the women are actually encouraged to go to the Catholic Worker house— The Mustard Seed—a few streets away. The Mustard Seed serves a full meal at 6 p.m., and those at the shelter are understandably not anxious to be duplicating services in the neighborhood. The challenge is big enough as is—and sometimes adventuresome.

Rafferty does not live on the edge of danger, but she concedes that once or twice she has had close calls.

"In the early days of the shelter," she says, "a woman came in with a bag and carried it upstairs. She had a pint of vodka. Sometimes liquor puts people to sleep, and they sleep calmly all night. But this woman turned into a wild person. I went upstairs to calm her down, and she got a grip on me, around my neck, and I thought I was done for. Sister Elaine came up and was able to persuade her to let her hands go. The woman was probably more frightened than I, but she did get a good grip on me. Since that time we've been more careful. If anyone has a bag, I say, 'Why don't you leave it down here?' Because you never know what people are going to carry upstairs."

Another time a husband came after his wife, who had taken shelter following some family difficulty. He was refused entry, and in his rage he kicked the door in. "That big door was practically off its hinges," Rafferty remarks. "He became frightened at his own violence, however, and he ran off. We were very fortunate. Since then, we've had heavy bolts put on the door."

There is no evangelizing or proselytizing at the shelter. "The religion we offer is very earthy," Rafferty declares. "It's a warm bed. It's a couple of people who are really glad to see you. It's ears to listen and something to eat. And very often it's clothes to wear. Some women are concerned to know, 'Are you a sister or aren't you?' Most don't really care. They're just happy to have somebody who is kind and gentle and compassionate and sometimes firm. In the early days of the shelter a group from the Legion of Mary came very often with little cards, and we would leave them out on the table in case anyone wanted to pick them up. But basically, ourselves and our personal resources are what we offer as religion."

The reaction of the diocese to the fact of Abby's House has been interesting. There was no rebonding after the break between Rafferty and the diocesan Urban Ministry Commission, although she says she has reached back. "I think it's always been a touchy point that we founded the shelter separate from diocesan sponsorship," she comments. "I think it never occurred to them that we would do it. Still, I would have been willing to go along with the diocese if there had been any indication on that commission that they were really interested in acting."

Nevertheless the diocese has not been averse about claiming Abby's House. "We weren't open a year when they published a directory of resources available in the diocese," Rafferty notes, "and Abby's House was claimed as being a diocesan agency. We laugh about it now—how after the shelter was started it got to be claimed. But, as I said, in the beginning nobody really wanted to get serious about it. That's a whole other issue to think about. Anyway, we're claimed but only very indirectly acknowledged."

And, until recently, when it was claimed it was as *Abbey's* House, as if the shelter acquired institutional respectability by bearing the name of some kind of monastic dwelling. In point of fact the shelter is named after Abigail Kelley Foster—popularly known as Abby—a Worcester woman who was involved in the 19th-century Abolitionist Movement with William Lloyd Garrison, and who was also associated with Elizabeth Cady Stanton and Susan B. Anthony in speaking out for women's rights.

Why Abigail Kelley Foster? Because the shelter was opened in the Bicentennial Year, when people were recovering the histories of important historical figures. For Worcester, one was Abby Foster. "She died just around the corner from here," explains Rafferty, "and we thought, 'Oh, what a great thing it would be to keep her memory alive in Worcester by having women, maybe equally as committed to women's rights, open a shelter and name it after her.'" So they called theirs the Abby Kelley Foster Home—until social agencies started arriving at the door with children little and big, believing from the name Foster that this was literally a foster home. To eliminate confusion, the Abby Kelley Foster Home became simply Abby's House.

All this is, of course, a long way from Rafferty's religious yesterdays—although she disputes this to a degree. She still feels very connected to teaching, since many sisters of her congregation who are still in the apostolate of teaching come to Abby's House and the Worcester Connection to observe and sometimes to help staff. "So the shelter and the center have served as a school of sorts," Rafferty argues. "It isn't like a school where you sit at a desk and learn. But many women who are in traditional apostolates are coming here and have learned some new way, perhaps, to be sensitive to kids in their own classrooms, who may be products of the broken families they see here."

Also, she feels very connected to her order, serving on the vocational education board and being affiliated with a Sisters of St. Joseph convent in Worcester. Still, her choice is to live among the women she has come to consider her extended family. "This neighborhood and these women are a part of me," she says, "and I don't want to separate myself from them, not at this point in my life."

Yet there is in her situation a double paradox at work. The first is that in living apart from her order Rafferty actually feels closer to it. She words it this way: "It's curious, but I have never felt more apostolically productive and at the same time more a part of the Sisters of St. Joseph than I do now. There's a mystery there. As I involve myself more with the human community of suffering women, I feel more at the heart of my own religious community. I haven't thought through what that means."

The second paradox is not unrelated to the first. It is that her lifestyle might actually be undercutting the order she loves so much, and the life she chose for herself as a young woman, by providing a kind of model for the new religious community of the 1980s and 1990s. The possibility awes her, and concerns her. "I'm torn, because I feel there's a very important place in the future for women with vision and women who give their total life to their ministry. But I'm discovering more and more that this is not just—quote—religious nun woman—unquote. I work with single lay women, who are as committed to ministry as I am. I am working with a married couple, who are building a family and are as committed to the issues as I am. I really don't know what to say. I don't see the community of the future being one of religious women exclusively. I see it as a religious body of people, maybe a couple of sisters, a married couple, maybe someone like one of our local priests who has had Latin American experience. In other words I envision something quite different from what we're now living: celibate women together. Now the celibate woman community may continue to have a valid place. But as I look to the future, I see religious communities surfacing in altogether new ways. We'll be living in much more integrated communities in the future."

In substance Rafferty envisions convent walls, already badly breached, coming down even more in the future.

And whereas others might not give a hoot, she is deeply worried.

"I'll tell you what worries me," she comments. "I'm concerned about the care of the sick and infirm, those sisters who gave their lives to the old models of church and who are now in our retirement homes and infirmaries. We're going to have to find ways of supporting them, so that they can die in peace and with care. That's a worry I have. I'm not forgetting those women; I'm very much aware of them. And I don't know how we're going to do for them all that we should."

Her other great worry is herself. "I suppose vision does keep you young," she says, "but I am occasionally aware that I'm in midlife. I'm over 50. I've got a lot of energy, but I'm not sure I'm going to continue to have that energy, and if I'm going to be able to continue to live out these visions. I'm not sure the body's going to keep up with them." Her prayer therefore is for good health—a lot of good health. "I've been blessed all my life," she comments, "but I'm honest enough to say that I have some real human worries. Anyway, I keep moving."

As she moves Rafferty feels a deep spiritual fulfillment, and she feels that God has been more real in her life as a religious since she began what she calls her "journey of conversion" in 1971. Not that God was not there before, and not that she was not connected to God in a very real way as teacher and later as facilitator. "It's rather that it's been more flesh and blood," she says. "Never in all my years have I felt more in touch with my own humanity. And since I definitely believe the kingdom of God is in the guts, I guess I have never been more aware of my own apostolic spirituality. I've never been so challenged. I've never had to let go of so much. I've never had to do so much redefining of vows. I've never had to question myself more than in the past several years. Like, why do you stay? What is it that makes religious life still work for you? When you find yourself confronted with situations that make you question, then it's a good place to be. Because in confronting questions you remain authentic."

Annette Rafferty is obviously a happy woman. Still, things bug her about the church, most especially what she terms the "structural injustice" done women. "In the early 1970s I became interested in ordination," she explains. "I felt that ordination was where it was at—that if women could be ordained, equality in the church perhaps would come about. I'm not saying that that still isn't somewhere in the back of my head, but I'm more convinced now that the sexism in the structures is what we have to organize around, rather than ordination. Our inability to be ordained is symptomatic of the greater problem of being excluded."

She is particularly annoyed with the sexist language of the church, recent improvements notwithstanding. "Either I am named what I am not—a brother, man—or I am not named at all," she comments. "I am at a point in my life where I don't want to be named what I am not, and I feel so much of my own ministry through what I have been able to do here with other women that I resent not being named at all." She says she feels this annoyance acutely in her parish participation. (She stays connected to a parish because she wants never to separate herself from the grassroots church.) For instance, she likely would have trouble being a Confraternity of Christian Doctrine teacher for the same reason that she eventually had trouble

77

teaching in a school classroom. "I couldn't continue teaching," she remarks, "because I do not believe women have full participation in the church. Like presenting Confirmation to youths as a step to full participation. It's not real. To have full participation in the sacramental system of the church, seven sacraments have to be available to all the people. But only six are available to women! I find that structural injustice so much more than I can bear that I cannot even mouth full participation."

Yet if Holy Orders were available to her, Rafferty is not certain she would take them. "I love church," she says, "and I love being part of church. But I would have to say that as the institutional church is operating now—in clerical fashion—I would not be interested in being part of that system. On the other hand I feel very much as though I am experiencing Orders. I feel my own priesthood very much without being in the clerical cast." How far does the feeling carry? Does it carry to the liturgical altar, as with some women who have been featured in the national press? The feeling stops short of that, it would seem, although a room of the Worcester Connection has been used for women's liturgies. There kindred souls will gather on occasion to conduct a worship service, which is described as "a free-flowing way of sharing a poem, a dance, a reading, and then possibly—symbolically—sharing bread and wine as a commitment to each other."

As for the future, Rafferty has hope mixed with fear. She thinks it is urgent for religious women to beware the trap of redefining themselves as separate or different from other women in the world. "We are not separate," she says. "I don't know how we ever became so institutionalized, when we were so free-flowing in our early communities." She is hopeful that real change is in process.

The fear is that the day is fast coming when Rome will require religious communities to choose between canonical and noncanonical status. "If it's canonical status," she speculates, "we'll be opting to go back to the flesh pots of Egypt. We'll be discontinuing the journey. I get scared about that, because I'd hate to make a decision to leave the people who mean so much to me."

The key to her reading of the immediate future is, of course, Pope John Paul II, and he leaves her with ambiguous emotions. "I get real scared," she sums up, "when I study objectively what is happening in Rome, and what appears to be John Paul II's approach to life. We have some tough years ahead; we're going to have to make some very serious decisions within the next few years. Unless, that is, the assassination attempt on his life gave him a chance to reflect and he comes out of the experience thinking altogether differently. But I tend to think that's not going to happen. I can't say that I don't care about him, because I do. But, oh, I just don't think that what works in Warsaw is going to work in Worcester."

4

Beating Swords Into Plowshares

Sister Anne Montgomery, R.S.C.J., is a most unlikely peace activist. In fact she's almost a stereotype of the average American sister: soft of voice, gentle of manner, modest to the core, retiring. Certainly she is not the one you would pick out of a roomful of nuns to slip into an arms plant and be party to the hammering of nuclear missiles on their way to the military. Yet there she was as one of the Plowshares 8, the peace activist group which entered the General Electric Co. plant at King of Prussia, Pa. on Sept. 9, 1980, splashed human blood around and scattered ashes over tools and documents, and banged dents into the nose cones of two Minuteman 3 Intercontinental Ballistic Missiles—this in answer to the biblical summons of the prophets Isaiah and Micah to beat swords into plowshares.

I talked with Montgomery in the parlor of the house of prayer that is home on Washington Square North in the Greenwich Village section of Manhattan Island. She was awaiting the trial in Norristown, Pa. that would find her and the other seven Plowshares members guilty as charged on major counts. Before our meeting she had just been released on bail after being held 11 weeks in jail, and, though she had no idea at the time, she would subsequently be sentenced to a term of one-and-a-half to five years in prison, a stiff sentence that of course would be appealed, together with the conviction. She knew that in the coming trial anything could happen, that judge and jury could be as tough as her prosecuting attorneys. But thoughts of the worst did not faze her. She *was* a remarkably composed woman. And *is*.

Anne Montgomery was born in San Diego in 1926, and entered the Religious of the Sacred Heart in 1948. She taught for the better part of two decades in schools of her order in the East, generally at the high-school level. Then in 1969 her vocation took a turn. She resigned her post at the Academy of the Sacred Heart on 91st Street in New York City for studies at Hunter College and a career of work with the poor. The next five years were spent at a street academy in Albany, followed by a year in Los Angeles for an internship at the Frostig Center, a school for children with learning disabilities whose program is coordinated with the graduate school at Mount St. Mary's College, followed by three years back in New York, in East Harlem, where she ran a resource room for learning disabilities at Mt. Carmel/Holy Rosary School.

It seems a long leap from a schoolroom, even a schoolroom in East Harlem, to the action in King of Prussia, but Montgomery argues that was no leap at all. And indeed by her recounting it is all quite logical. "Working with children and the disadvantaged, and in Albany with street kids having such a hard time getting basic services, I began to see how much of the money in our society, how much of the concern was not going where it was needed," she comments. "They were going to arms build-up, and very possibly another horrifying war."

During the Vietnam war Montgomery was not an activist. Hers was a semi-cloistered community before Vatican II, which meant that members did not leave the convent for anything but medical or educational purposes. "I didn't have that interaction with people who were really involved that would make me feel that I just had to act," she explains. "I could talk about peace. I could teach children about peace and justice. I felt that was my mission." As she moved around more after the Council, came in contact with people who were more directly concerned and active, she learned how devastating the arms race was to what should have been national social priorities. She decided there was no reason for not speaking out and acting herself.

Admittedly she left an important work. It is not every person who is available to work in East Harlem, and fewer still who have the skills to run a resource room for learning disabilities. Montgomery left a gap behind her in East Harlem, for the school could not find another teacher to replace her. Accordingly, the work does not go on, and that pains her. But for Montgomery it was a case of weighing one urgency against another. She concluded that the nuclear arms crisis was these children's crisis as much as anyone else's. "They're not going to grow up if we have a nuclear war," she declares. "They are living in a neighborhood where there are burnt-out buildings. There's glass falling into their playgrounds. And money is being withdrawn from the cities and from the poor to fund this arms race. It's crazy. So it's the same crisis in the end. Those children are suffering now. As popes and others have said, the arms race kills the poor even before we have a war. That very thing is happening."

Thus it was that Montgomery figured that she had to

take the risk of witness. "I did have a responsibility to my children in Harlem," she says, "but still I was something extra in the school. I was doing learning disabilities. The regular classes would go on if I wasn't there. I felt that their lives were more important than whatever I could give them for one or two years in the way of teaching. Their lives were already threatened because of the environment in which they lived. So I felt that in joining in the King of Prussia action, and facing prison perhaps, I wasn't giving up on my responsibilities to these children. Rather it was a way of fulfilling them."

It was Daniel Berrigan, the Jesuit activist, who inspired, or at least eased, Montgomery's move into the witnessing community for peace—as he has so many others. Berrigan is not a proselytizer or evangelizer for activism, as some might think. His method is to lay out the facts, and then let the facts motivate the person. In other words he did not pressure Montgomery to her witness. She attended a series of meditations that Berrigan was giving on the Book of Revelation at the house of prayer on 97th Street, and in the course of one of them he mentioned that peace demonstrations were occurring in Washington. Montgomery decided to go to a meeting about one of them, thinking to herself, "Well, I'm not going to get involved, but I at least ought to hear what it's about." She left that meeting persuaded that one *had* to be involved; that one *had* to speak out against the arms race; that as an individual one could do all sorts of things, even if it was only pass out leaflets or hold up a banner.

Her baptism of activism came in the spring of 1978 and that year's United Nations Disarmament Session. She walked in the demonstration peace marches on the U.N., and she took part in the June 12 sit-in. These things she found easy to do, as there were no severe penalties attached to the actions. But the stakes were on the table, and the ante went up. Montgomery stayed.

That summer she went to one of the seminar/workshops that Philip Berrigan, the former Josephite priest, and his wife Elizabeth McAlister, herself once a Religious of the Sacred Heart, conduct at the resistance-community center in Baltimore they call Jonah House. She thought "it would be a good way to learn a little more about myself." She went and was impressed with their nonviolence—"not only the nonviolence of their actions and their speaking, but also of their lifestyle." She discovered a new sense of community.

To get to know one another and to form community, participants joined in what therapists call life-sharing. There was education on the arms race. They learned facts, saw movies, explored their own religious history, and drew out the symbols that were most meaningful to them. They "vigiled" at the Pentagon. "The depth of that procedure; the fact that nobody was being pushed to do civil disobedience; that everyone was allowed to do what he or she felt easy with; that everyone had a part; that the procedure drew on our religious tradition—all this appealed to me," Montgomery says. "It was not an exercise of superficial thought or action, or angry speaking out. It was done with meaning and love and true nonviolence." In any case the experience really hooked Montgomery into the peace movement.

Back in New York she joined in the leafleting and other actions at Riverside Research Institute, a Pentagon think-tank. She prayed and she studied, and she kept her ties to Jonah House, going to Washington at Christmastide for Jonah House's annual Pentagon demonstration on the feast of the Massacre of the Holy Innocents, and returning during Holy Week and in the summer.

It was through these contacts that Montgomery learned about the projected King of Prussia action. One of the men approached her and inquired if she would be interested in performing an action that would involve destruction of property and might have very serious penalties. She didn't impulsively say yes. She felt she had to pray and think about her decision—and find out more about the action. Nothing in this process persuaded her that she should not participate. Then when Molly Rush, director of the Thomas Merton Center in Pittsburgh and the mother of several children, announced that she "was in," Montgomery felt she had no excuse in the world for not acting. "It was very important to have at least two women involved," she says, "as it's hard for someone to go to jail for a long time the first time alone. And neither of us had spent more than a night in jail. I had spent one night in a Washington jail at one point, but that was all."

So the planning took place; the worries were thrashed out. "We were very concerned that the public understand that we were nonviolent," Montgomery recalls. "We planned to hide hammers under our clothes and use them on the missiles, and as soon as people think of hammers, they think of violence. We wanted to make it very clear that this was a symbolic act, and that the hammers were to be used on the missiles only, and not on any people."

The rest is history. The action took place; the activists were arrested on the spot. Did Montgomery have misgivings or afterthoughts of regret? Not at all. "Personally, I had come to the point where I believed that if there was a chance to dismantle a missile, it was the thing to do," she says. "I felt it was the strongest means of communicating what we felt everyone should be doing: taking missiles apart. It was what should be done." Montgomery admits to having been strongly influenced by activist-writer James Douglass and a point he made about Jonestown, the cult commune that came to its disastrous end in 1978 with the cyanide suicides/murders of more than 900 men, women, and children. Douglass related the nuclear threat to Jonestown's vats of cyanide, and he asked, What would have happened if somebody had tipped over those vats of cyanide? That terrible death scene would never have taken place. Douglass then likened missiles and nuclear storage places to those vats of cyanide and demanded, "What are we going to do about it?

"His question was very much in my mind," says Montgomery. "If one of those missiles could be taken apart as a message of what should happen, then we should do it."

Hers sounds like a remarkably independent action—which it was. But it was not an action entered into in defiance of the prayerful good order of the Religious of the Sacred Heart, nor in some selfish spirit of self-fulfillment. "I hate the word fulfillment," she says. "Our fulfillment is up to God." She strives rather to be faithful. "There are many calls in our life, and I try very hard to listen. It was hard before the King of Prussia action to say, 'Am I really meant to do this at this moment in my life? Was it the best way I could meet my responsibilities?' We have those choices all along, and I want to be obedient in the way I listen. I check out with my own religious vocation, with my superiors, whatever, so that I am aware of what God wants me to do. There's a lot of room for choices in there, and it doesn't mean that because one choice is right, the other is necessarily wrong." She argues that to focus on fulfillment makes it seem as if that were the goal of religious life. "And I don't think it is," she adds, "although I think it will happen somewhere along the line. We find the fullness of God in our lives and in our prayer even when we don't feel it."

So Montgomery did not fly recklessly into the King of Prussia action. She discussed it with her superiors to the extent that this was possible—partly, as she said, to "check out"; and partly to be honest with an essential element in nonviolence, which is that people be perfectly open about what they are doing. Her provincial had encouraged her in the peace work, even recommending that she have only a part-time job so that she would be freer to be engaged in the movement. At the same time, the provincial asked Montgomery to let her know beforehand if she was going to perform an action that might risk prison. Thus confidences were shared before the King of Prussia action, with only those details held back which, if bandied about, could compromise the action. (Reserve was also dictated by considerations that too much information shared could make the party or parties receiving the information an accessory before the fact and thus, in the legal sense, an accomplice.) "I told my provincial I was going to do something that would involve greater risk than before, and perhaps a long jail term," she says. "Of course, we've been carrying on a dialogue about it ever since."

Did she receive encouragement or discouragement? Montgomery claims encouragement. Some of her co-religious had trouble with the King of Prussia action, but she gives them credit for being "very open" about listening to why she did what she did. Many have changed their minds since.

"But there was something more," Montogmery adds. "Our mother general from Rome was visiting in the United States, and the week I was released from jail on bail, which was Thanksgiving week, she happened to be in New York. Of all weeks for her to be here! I knew she was supportive in the past, but I was amazed at the degree of her support now. She had no problem with the action at all. I think it was because she's traveled so much to different countries—including Latin America—and so she knows what's going on." By which Montgomery meant that she has seen poverty and is sensitive to the degree to which the arms race keeps so much of the world poor, desperately poor. Thus, the mother general was "totally supportive," and Montgomery found that a great help.

Still there are those questions as old as Catonsville and other assertions against the military mentality. Are not actions like King of Prussia passé, a reliving of the Vietnam era, a stubborn refusal to let go of yesterday? And passé or not, are not such actions self-defeating, since jail takes the witnessers out of circulation and neutralizes their witness at least for the length of the sentence? Montgomery's answers are a combination of impatience and disagreement.

The people who raise the passé issue are passé themselves, she counters. She does not try to answer them. "I leave the answering to people who were involved during the Vietnam era. The people who are asking that question are stuck in the era themselves. An action that speaks against death is never passé. A symbolic action is always valid. A nonviolent action is always valid, whether in Gandhi's India or our United States. Because some of the same people happen to be acting now who acted during the Vietnam years invalidates nothing. I say 'Thank God.' The nuclear threat is so horrible and so threatening to life on earth! What we're doing has nothing to do with the 1960s, except that killing people is always wrong."

She then offers a testimonial to the resisters of the '60s, who continue to resist: "I admire people like the Berrigans, like John Bach of Hartford, a draft resister, and others whom I have met who were involved in the '60s. That they have not gone on to other things; that they see this threat of genocide, of homicide growing worse and worse; that they live their lives to speak for life—that's a great thing. Some of these people live in community. They serve the poor. They make their living painting houses or moving furniture, or whatever way they can. And they work for peace. It's to be admired that they stick it out."

On the question of jailing, Montgomery is firm, though less intense. "In a sense you're hidden," she says, "but it will be worth it. People are conscious that others have gone to prison for this, and consider it worthwhile. They're conscious that jailing is what happens in this country when people speak out in a strong way for peace and against the government policy." The echo of the Berrigans rings through the words. "We're a reminder to people."

"People constantly ask about the effectiveness of what we do," Montgomery continues. "They say, 'What is the use of going to jail? You're out of circulation for a long time.' I say, it was part of Gandhi's tradition of nonviolence, and of Christ's, that you don't talk about effectiveness too much. You'd like people to listen, but you have to speak the truth, and you have to do the right thing and let the consequences take care of themselves. Obviously you try to act in such a way as to communicate, and certainly we tried to communicate with the King of Prussia action. Did we communicate? There's been a great response from people all over the country, all sorts of little people, I'd say. They seem to have understood."

Typical of the New Nun—a designation she hates incidentally, for reasons I will get to later—Montgomery's life as a sister has gone through some dramatic evolutions. Basically she ascribes it to a sensitizing on her part to the needs of the poor and the deprived. "Our schools were doing a good job," she says, "and they're doing a better job now. But I began to see that there were many children, especially in New York City, who needed good teaching and simply weren't getting it." This led to a transition year, which she spent at Hunter College on a fellowship aimed at helping teachers become leaders in their schools in changing curriculum and in helping children below grade level in reading and language arts. She learned much and put the learning to use.

Then she heard of a street academy, which Sister Maryellen Harmon of her order was organizing in Albany to pick up those dropouts whose "school" was the streets. It was to be a real academic school, so that youngsters could get back into other schools or even into college. Montgomery taught English, ran a learning laboratory for five years, and lived in a housing project called Green Street in the south end of the city. "The south end is one of the poorest parts of Albany," she says, "and we were interested in working with the poor and living among the poor." The reason is elementary: "We have more to learn from people who are poor and struggling with poverty than we sometimes have to give them."

A year followed at the Frostig Center in Los Angeles, where Montgomery received her certification in learning disabilities. Then it was to East Harlem, where she ran the resource room in learning disabilities at Mt. Carmel/Holy Rosary School. Once again she was up close to the poor. She felt satisfied, and in conformity with the tradition of her order. When the Religious of the Sacred Heart arrived in the United States from France, the 19th century was well advanced and the American Catholic parochial school system was in place, serving by and large the immigrant poor. The religious of the Sacred Heart had been founded in the very class-conscious time after the French Revolution, when in France schools for the poor were quite separate from schools for the rich and the well-to-do. But the order's founder, Sister Madeleine Sophie Barat, insisted that for every school her order opened for the upper classes, there should be one opened at the same time for the poor. The order evolved differently in the United States, precisely because Catholic schools for the poor already existed. The Religious of the Sacred Heart, therefore, became more identified with schools for the middle class and the wealthy. Yet the old tradition was never lost, and when the loosening up came after Vatican II, many sisters of the order were able to explore new ways of working with the poor, thus restoring in this country the society's history of working with people of various classes.

Montgomery, of course, was one of them. Still, she says,

she feels something of a hypocrite. "We talk about the poor," she explains, "but it's very hard for us to say that we can ever completely identify ourselves with the poor when we have a choice to do something else. The poor don't have that freedom. That's a very big difference. Like I'm living here now on Washington Square North, which is far from a poor place—although we try to live a very simple life. I'm living here because the prayer life is so important and because I think the work being done here to help people pray is vital. It's essential, really, to the conversion of the city—you know, people living a life of prayer and helping other people to pray, especially people in ministries among city people. Whatever, I have many choices that the poor people don't have."

Montgomery lives in a house of prayer called Aletheia along with five sisters of other congregations. The Sisters of Charity own the building, and one of the members of the Aletheia group is Sister of Charity Eileen Storey, a key figure in the growth of houses of prayer in the New York area. She was assigned by the Sisters of Charity to study the house of prayer movement about 12 years ago as a way of helping revitalize the prayer life of sisters and bringing a little more space into their busy lives. In the years since she has been involved in helping to found several houses of prayer, all of them intercommunity. Storey is very interested in what Eastern prayer has to say to the Western church, and accordingly she spent a year in India, visiting various ashrams, talking to people, and praying in that silent meditation that makes use of the Jesus prayer, breathing, and yoga. As Montgomery comments, "She wanted to bring back to this country and recombine with our tradition something we always had but sometimes haven't used much: the richness of silent meditation or contemplation."

Those who joined Aletheia stress contemplation. They meditate together for an hour in the morning. They pray together at night, or have a liturgy. And they welcome others to what they call their school of prayer with emphasis on Scripture, prayer, social concern, and meditation. Montgomery sees advantages in her Washington Square North location: "The transportation here is very easy. All the subways run down here. People can come here with a sense of arriving and getting home again in relative safety. It's not easy to find a place in the city where you have all that, and at a price you can meet. This was just a gift." She is grateful to the Sisters of Charity, landlord, and a supporter of their interest in houses of prayer.

This is actually Montgomery's second house of prayer. Previously she was with the group at Covenant House, the crisis center for runaways, street kids, and children caught in the pornographic district around Times Square. Covenant House is the apostolate begun by Franciscan Father Bruce Ritter, which has grown into a huge operation, with a staff numbering in the hundreds and a volunteer corps of some 40 people. "Bruce leans on the strength of prayer," Montgomery says. "Also he wanted a place where volunteers at Covenant House could retreat and find a little peace during the day and be helped by joining in the prayer. So he found an apartment to be used in that way. I joined the second year. We lived in community. We prayed together. We had part-time jobs."

It is by the jobs of its members that houses of prayer subsist. Generally these jobs are part-time—enough to provide a living and pay expenses, while leaving time for prayer life and other apostolic involvements. Montgomery believes that houses of prayer may be harbingers of the future, certainly in the sense that they group sisters into small communities. Most of the co-religious of her congregation are living in small communities, and she thinks the mode is here to stay. "People are in alternate places and see their mission in alternate ways," she says. "It's a more realistic kind of life. Nobody's sending in a food service or taking care of expenses that you don't even know about. You have to plan and budget together. You have to plan your prayer life together. You have to be realistic." Small communities, in other words, contribute to the maturity of the individual religious woman, and in senses other than management. They also increase human contact by being located among neighborhood people. Eileen Storey says the ideal is a house of prayer on every block. This may be impossible, but the goal is challenging.

And so Sister Anne Montgomery lives her life, feeling very close to her roots because of Aletheia's and her order's emphasis on contemplation, and being convinced that she could not have joined in the action at King of Prussia without that source of prayer. She is happy and content and devoid of the distress some nuns feel because ordination is denied to them. "I certainly think women should be ordained," she remarks. "Men are. But I don't feel called to be one of them." She believes very strongly "in the priesthood of the faithful, and in the sharing of that priesthood." For her that is ample.

Finally, she rejects the notion that she is a so-called New Nun. The term bothers her, she says. "Sometimes when words like 'radical' and 'new' are used, they're meant to emphasize a break with the past. I like to think a lot of what I'm doing now is really in my own tradition, and it is certainly in the Christian tradition—a very ancient tradition of pacifism, and prayer, and ministry, which is never old and never new."

In more ways than one she is very likely right. For the New Nun is now more the norm than the new. They are up to daring and innovative things. It's just that not all of them are breaking into intercontinental missile plants.

5

A Latin in a Non-Latin Church

She sits opposite me in a desk chair in a classroom of Emmanuel College in Boston. The Fenway district is outside, and just down the block is the Red Sox baseball park, its ugly light arches reaching up like monster arms from a Japanese horror movie. She could be another of the tens of thousands of kids who have made Boston into College-town, U.S.A. She's that youthful looking. She could also be the queen of the prom, she's that attractive. But she's no kid, and she's no ballroom student. She is Sister Rosalinda Ramirez, 37, a Missionary Sister of the Sacred Heart. That's the order founded by St. Francis Xavier Cabrini, Mother Cabrini, the first American citizen to be canonized. Ramirez is an intensely serious person. She was at Emmanuel to direct a workshop of the National Assembly of Women Religious on the topic "A Lesson on Becoming a Prophet." The workshop I did not attend, but I concluded that if anyone could conduct such a session, it was she. Ramirez is something of a prophet herself. Prophets can be angry people. Ramirez is angry about several things: as a woman in a male chauvinist church; as a Latin in a non-Latin church. She speaks like a Jeremiah.

Sister Rosalinda Ramirez, M.S.S.H., is spiritual director

and retreat director at the Cabrini Retreat Center in Des Plaines, Ill. It is in this capacity that the first grievance is encountered—that of the church's predominantly male orientation. Ramirez gives group retreats; in 1973 she even conducted a retreat for priests of the Archdiocese of Boston. She also conducts private, directed retreats, including the Ignatian Exercises, for individuals. Inevitably she is handicapped in this work, specifically in terms of those who during the course of a retreat wish to have a traditional liturgical celebration or traditional reception of the Sacrament of Reconciliation. Because at that point she has to have a priest on hand; she has to invite in another person to satisfy the need of her retreatant. It is a circumstance that she finds an imposition on her, both as woman and religious. But more pertinently she finds it an imposition on the retreatants.

"The retreatants have spent five, six, seven, eight days with me," she says. "They have shared their innermost spiritual life, their personal life with me." Then they have to turn to someone else. "Most simply state that they are not willing to go through that again with another person, who comes in totally cold and totally foreign to their situation. I am the one with whom they want to be able to celebrate the sacraments, since it is with me that the relationship has developed. It is very cumbersome and difficult for them to have to shift gears all of a sudden, to have to sit down with a person who is a total stranger to them and go through a formal sacrament of reconciliation or celebration of the Eucharist." Her voice bristles.

Ramirez concedes that the outsider provides all that the technical and canonical letter of sacramentality demands. But gone is that sense of community, that sense of sharing which has built up over several days. It is painful, she says, for the retreatant, and again herself—"because I would like to have it accepted by the church that it is through me that the grace of God has brought this person to a point of reconciliation."

On the other hand there are retreatants who refuse to switch, and who join with Ramirez in what she calls paraliturgical ceremonies. For example, during the course of a retreat she will hear confessions.

In the early church it was common for Christians to confess to one another, priest or not, and that was the sacrament then. It is the point of reference for Ramirez's practice now. "Confession is part and parcel of the service, if you want to put it that way," she declares. "For persons to disclose their sins to me is just natural to the retreat experience. Now a person who is looking for a clerical exercising of the Sacrament of Reconciliation obviously will not get that from me—not in the present church. But if a person is looking for acceptance and exchange, profession, reconciliation, a praying together, the person can achieve these in this experience." Does Ramirez give a form of absolution? She answers, "I pray with the retreatant for forgiveness."

Similarly with respect to the Eucharist. "There are times when, symbolically, we do take the cup," she says. "There are times when we do break bread together. We pray together. We reflect on the Scriptures, particularly those passages relating to the Last Supper. We share what this means to each other, and we do have a prayerful experience."

Ramirez denies that there is anything defiant or "underground church" about these practices. "I don't tell people they have attended the Eucharist. I don't profess to perform the Consecration, so to speak. That would not be acceptable within the structure in which I am working at the retreat center. So I do not claim to do that. It is simply a paraliturgical celebration. In the early 1960s it might have been called an agape. I do not state that I have celebrated or am replacing the eucharistic celebration of the church. Now, whether I feel that way is one thing. But I do not so promote it to any retreatant."

The role of pseudo-priest is not one that Ramirez enjoys, so understandably she would take Holy Orders if the sacrament were available to her. She considers it an injustice that it is withheld. "It is a distortion that has crept into the development of the church, as have so many others. Distortions concerning religious life, concerning church, concerning sacraments, concerning so many things." She argues that "the most painful distortion" is that women cannot be ordained—"it's a mistake, it's a misconception."

Yet Ramirez lives in a changing church, and the seemingly impossible has occurred many times over, from the repeal of Friday abstinence to the replacement of Latin as the language of the liturgy. Might there be still another impossible change, this one allowing someone as young as Ramirez to live to see the day when she, a woman, could be ordained? Sometimes she says she is hopeful, other times not. "Who knows how long my lifetime will be?" she counters. Then she adds cogently: "I do believe as a woman of faith that if God has blessed me and called me to the breaking of bread and to reconciling, the will of God eventually will prevail. If there is a calling of women to the priesthood by God, it will happen no matter how hard the present structures might fight it. *It will happen.* The will of God will prevail in any test with the institution."

In the Episcopal Church, of course, one of the ways by which the barriers on women priests were broken was bishops' taking the ordination matter into their own hands and, as those uniquely empowered to confer the sacrament, going ahead and ordaining women. It is hard to imagine that happening in American Catholicism, but in the event that it did, would Ramirez kneel before the ordaining bishop? She says quite frankly that she doesn't know. "I couldn't tell you yes right now, and my reason is that I think the problem runs a lot deeper." The issue of women's ordination is a sign to the church, she argues—"a prophetic sign, if you will." But it is only one detail that needs to be challenged and revamped. There are positions and perceptions needing challenge which are much more fundamental. "For instance the exercise of ministry and the way in which hierarchy is conceived. I am much more interested in the revamping of the structure of the church and the relationship to its people, its clergy, its religious, its laity, than I am with simply being ordained into what exists," she says. The whole experience of church has to be entered into differently.

How does one go about making a different church? Ramirez has no magic formulas. She speaks only for herself: "What I see myself doing is speaking the truth as I see it and living as close as I can to the way I think things should be. In other words practicing what I believe should be practiced and accepting the fact that for that I pay the price. I believe that's the only way change occurs. There are people who can walk into institutions and begin working with them. I say that is definitely one way to assist.

However, I don't believe that can be successful by itself. It is also essential to have people who are willing to live what should be lived, and who stand as a contradiction to what is and an invitation to what should be."

Rosalinda Ramirez has stood in contradiction, to use her phrase. She has challenged diocesan positions in open forum; she has worked with the poor and oppressed and denounced church structures for having a type of relationship with them that she did not consider just; she has been involved in demonstrations and sit-ins and been lugged indecorously away by police, until now always just short of arrest and jail. (Jail is not exactly something one runs after, she comments.) She has spoken out against American policy in El Salvador and corporate exploitation of the Third World. Her sincerity, her love for the church, her religious congregation, her own religious life, are accepted as genuine. However, her activities do cause what she describes as alienation and misunderstanding, and that has cost her in terms of career and apostolate.

For instance, Catholic Theological Union in Chicago recently had a position open for director of the ministerial program in the Hispanic apostolate. Ramirez was invited to make an evaluation of Hispanic ministerial programs in the United States and to offer suggestions on how universities can better prepare people for Hispanic ministries. She did so very honestly from her perspective as a Hispanic herself and her experience with Hispanic ministries for several years all over the country. Hers was a stimulating report, which was presented orally and in writing to the Union. But it was also provocative. Thus, when a committee of students asked the search committee to send her an application for the position, the answer from the committee was, "No, she would be too radical for the administration; she would make them uncomfortable."

Other examples would be within her own congregation. "I think the majority of our sisters, particularly our leadership, neither understand nor comprehend where I'm coming from," Ramirez says quite frankly. "They work in structures I do not work in, and often I am involved in protests or in speaking out against positions so that their interests come under fire, indirectly if not directly. They find that very painful and cannot fit it into their understanding of my being in the congregation." Therefore there seems a great hesitancy in putting her in positions of authority within the congregation. She offers an example: "Let's say sisters recommend me to the board of trustees of our hospitals. Leadership persons respond that I am not supportive of institutional, corporate types of things and therefore it would not be comfortable to have me on that board."

There are other prices, Ramirez adds, "like slander, the loss of old friends, et cetera. One almost gets used to it, but never completely."

Is it fair criticism that she is indeed not temperamentally constituted to work in corporate or institutional-type situations? Ramirez does not mind the question. "It all depends on what you want from a person in that position," she answers. "If you want a yes-person, the answer is no, I am not constituted to be in that position. If you want someone who will be objectively critical, whose main focus will be the Christian element in that institution and not the profit margin, which is obviously a very important factor with a corporation and an institution, then you could say yes. I would be a very critical person. To me, institutions serve people, and when institutions fail to serve the needs of people, I find no use for them."

Rosalinda Ramirez was born in Wilmington, Del. and did most of her growing up in New York City. But she calls Maricao, Puerto Rico home. It is where she has spent much time and where her parents live. "I was raised and educated here," she reflects, "but I was raised and educated by parents who have a Hispanic mind. I grew up Puerto Rican. I never thought of being anything else, and I still don't." It is an ethnic pride that makes Ramirez a militant on Hispanic issues, particularly as these relate to American Catholicism. She believes that Hispanics are second-class members of the American church, and that annoys her. "When you single out a particular group of people, and you speak of dealing with their particular problems, then you're automatically making the assumption that they're not part of the original whole. So the Hispanic, yes, is a second-class member of the church." The blame she ascribes to the mind set of the American church. She develops her theory.

"I was on the ad hoc committee for the Hispanic Secretariat of the U.S. Catholic Conference. I don't want to say that the hierarchy of the official church is not sincere. Perhaps it is. But I think it is highly mistaken in much of what it perceives and does. One of the basic problems is the mind of the American church. It's an American-European mind, really, and it is quite different from the American-Hispanic mind." Her contention is that the two mentalities function out of a totally different set of priorities, and until the predominant mind set allows room for the other to exist as a fully legitimate, honorable ethnic and cultural entity, then the one will be regarded as superior and the other inferior. Ramirez explains the mind set complexity in terms of concepts of community and concepts of individual rights.

"When a Hispanic speaks of freedom, or of action, or conceives of something in relation to society, it is automatically assumed—if our Spanish perspective has not been usurped by a North American influence—that he or she is speaking about the community," she says. "We function out of a basic community mentality. We have a sense of understanding of the rights of people as a total communal concept. We do not have a clear understanding of the rights of the individual. That is something that we pick up when we come to this country. In the Hispanic context the individual exists for the community."

In the United States, according to her theory, it is pretty much the reverse. It is the individual who is the focus. "North Americans have an extremely clear concept of the individual's rights. But the North American does not know how to incorporate that into total societal laws. He does not think out of a societal or communal context. He thinks essentially out of the individual context and then applies that to the community and society." It is one reason, she contends, why there is such difficulty in the United States deciding on societal laws, societal guidelines, and community rights as opposed to individual rights. A whole different set of presumptions is at work concerning rights, needs, and justice.

The church, she maintains, falls victim to the mind set. "It shouldn't, because the church is a community. The hierarchy is not the church—the bishops are the servants of the church. The church is the community—the believers at large. We should therefore be functioning out of a community context. But the American church is saddled with the North American mind. The hierarchy does not know how to perceive the larger reality of the church, the community of believers, as opposed to individual laws and functions, or the individual parish as opposed to the total church reality."

The consequence is second-class status for Hispanics—and other minority ethnic groups, which have their own difficulties within the church. Ramirez does not presume to speak for them, but she does speak forcefully of and for Hispanics. She argues that much of the good that has been done for Hispanic Catholics in the American church has resulted from the efforts of Hispanic Catholics themselves and has been achieved "in spite of the local institutional church." Her words: "It has been done by laity, as well as by religious and some clergy, who have given themselves to servicing the people, drawing them together in basic communities—*comunidades de base*—small gatherings where people can think together and function together, where they can share their faith, interpret their history, and find their experience within their understanding of God, and where they believe God is leading them."

Unfortunately not all Hispanic Catholics in the United States have had the opportunity of drawing together in such communities; perhaps not even the majority. But many have, and it apparently has become a very important experience in their lives. "It has become a way of keeping in touch and nurturing church identity," Ramirez summarizes. "And that is something that is taking place outside the local institutional church."

What could the institutional church be doing to correct the situation regarding Hispanics? It is a question that Rosalinda Ramirez says is hard not to answer superficially, but she tries. "For one thing the Hispanic population needs its own people. It is important to allow Hispanic women and men to rise out of their own people, their own communities—and to service those communities." She considers it a travesty that Hispanic clergy should have to go through a non-Hispanic seminary training. "They learn a theology and acquire an outlook on life that has no relation to their historical or religious perspectives," she argues. "The North American seminary is highly influenced by North American culture. These men come out and they are not prepared to work with people who are totally from a Hispanic frame of reference. They are prepared to impose a cultural interpretation on a religious perspective that is not theirs."

Yet it is a fact that some Hispanics have risen to high places in the American church, including a number in the hierarchy. Ramirez is not persuaded that this means much. "They still have to walk a thin line between the delicate relationships with their people—if they remain faithful to the people—and the hierarchical clergy, who have a de facto understanding of what it means to be a bishop or priest coming out of a particular North American-European cultural milieu," she says. "That's a disastrous thing. It destroys our clergy; they become what they are not. It destroys our religious—for religious congregations do the same type of thing. They do not feel a responsibility to provide Hispanic vocations with Hispanic studies and missioning." Although a few religious congregations have made strides in new directions, the adage still applies she says: "To be a good religious is to be Anglicized or Europeanized."

Ramirez sees no easy resolution to the problem of the American church's incorporating of Hispanics into its very being. "You're dealing with an issue as fundamental as when you say, 'How does the hierarchy incorporate women into the priesthood?' You're talking about a fundamental change in self-understanding, in perception, in formation. You're talking about a whole different posture towards the world, towards society, towards God." It's not a case of just moving chess pieces across a board and putting them in different squares. It's a case of significant change in several behavioral, intellectual, and attitudinal areas.

Change will have to come, or, as Ramirez puts it, "some separate realities are going to develop." She is vague on the point, but it seems apparent that she is talking of the Hispanic population's going its own ecclesiastical way in the United States, and maybe even becoming what in pre-Vatican II days would be known as a schismatic church. Such a development could have disastrous effects on American Catholicism, if only because of the numbers involved. Hispanics now comprise up to one third of the total American Catholic population, and in cities such as New York and Miami Hispanics are rapidly becoming the predominant numerical element. Obviously it is essential that they continue to be part of the Catholic establishment.

Ramirez concedes that pastorals and other papers have been published which evidence great conceptual understandings of the situation. But she feels they are only promising of developments to come and not in themselves hard indicators that change is here. The developments had better come, and come soon, she says, else "there will be ruptures" that will force change. She does not look forward to that day.

What will allay confrontation? "The grace of God, working a conversion of heart and mind within the church." Her hope, however, is tinged with pessimism. "Too often conversions come about only through stress situations," she declares. "One example would be Latin America. Yet the church in Latin America did have a conversion of heart and mind, and now it stands in strong opposition to certain realities: the junta in El Salvador, the North American political structure, the administration in Washington. A conversion of heart and mind in the United States is going to be uncomfortable for a lot of people. What is going to allay that? Nothing will make it easy. Conversion does not come easily; a change that is fundamental never comes easily."

At the time of our conversation much of Ramirez's activity was given over to Central America and particularly the situation in El Salvador, where missionaries were being harassed, and where the four women missionaries, three of them religious, were murdered in December, 1980, a brutality that shocked the world. Her purpose essentially was to help raise the consciousness of the American public to what was happening in El Salvador: what the confrontation was about; what role the United States was playing in events there; what the position of the church was. "The American population is basically a good population," she commented. "It was important that they know the facts of El Salvador so that the United States government does not take a position contrary to the mind and hearts of the

American people." Like others working for the same cause, she hopes to bring pressure on Washington to adopt policies which are "much more in harmony with Christian truth."

Ramirez is totally supportive of the missionaries in El Salvador and bitter towards those, in Washington and in corners of the Catholic press, who level criticism at them, at the Maryknollers in particular, for allegedly crossing the fine line between apostolic witness and political activity. That is word usage, she maintains, which purely and simply is meant to inflame people and make them hostile to those whose only objective is to promote social justice and do good.

She is vehement on the point: "If I am in a country and you are poor, and I am binding your wounds, and I am feeding you, and I am sharing Scriptures with you, and I am praying with you and celebrating liturgical sacraments with you, helping you to maintain your life, and there's open conflict in your country, and in that open conflict you are not on the side of the existing junta, a junta that is known and can be proved to be violently repressive to its people, what happens? I become the enemy of those in power. I am there feeding you, and binding your wounds, and caring for you, supporting your hope and dignity. All of a sudden what were corporal and spiritual acts of mercy become political acts. People need to understand that."

In some respects it comes down to whose ox is being gored. Or, as Ramirez would have it, "when my activity becomes uncomfortable for your political interests, well then my ministry becomes a political activity for you."

She laments the distortion, nevertheless she concedes that those who raise the political involvement question may have a point. There may be a political dimension, although it should not necessarily keep people from acting. "I have only one life," she remarks. "If my perspective is Christian then my Christian consciousness will exercise itself in all arenas of my life, including the political arena. Politics is *not* above God. It would like to be. That's what 'crossing religious and political lines' implies—the phrase, that is. Too many fall for it."

The latter comments might appear to frame Ramirez in an essentially political context, but she would say otherwise. "For me, my basic life is my faith life, my life in Christ. I try to live that as honestly as I can. I'm not saying that I don't make mistakes. I'm open to that. But a mistake is a mistake, and life goes on. So I don't disqualify myself or my views on life and faith by any mistakes I have made, am making, or will make in the future." That would be unreal. "As a Christian I have no problem with making mistakes," she says, "because I believe essentially in the faith and in the forgiveness of Christ."

So she works—and she prays. In fact all her activity involves prayer, she maintains. Her reasoning is interesting: "Prayer is an openness, a desire, a willingness to be sensitive to the spirit within us. Because it is the spirit within us that cries out, that calls us to prayer. And when we cannot pray, it is the spirit within us that prays for us, and eventually brings us to prayer."

How exactly does she pray? That, she says, is like asking how one feeds a computer and with what? "Prayer is not that easily dealt with. It's not exactly *a thing* that one does." Her prayer life and her life in Christ have been developing over 37 years. "For me, Christ is with me always," she continues. "The spirit for me is something tangible and alive. I would say that at this point I may be praying always, because I depend on that spirit for my judgments and my perceptions. I can't say that I go to prayer. But prayer has found me, and praying is something I may be doing always. I may be doing it during this interview. I am not saying that my interview is a prayer. What I am saying is that in the course of this interview I have prayed."

Rosalinda Ramirez thus integrates prayer into her very being. There are times obviously when she withdraws totally to be in what she calls "dialogue with the spirit, or at least to rest in its presence." That would be her quiet time, her time away from others. But it does not mean that when she is out picketing at a nuclear arms demonstration, or driving to a migrant workers camp, or sitting in the office of a task force on El Salvador, or attending a conference of the National Assembly of Women Religious that she is not at the same time seriously attempting to maintain that dialogue, that relationship inside of her. "It is something that I depend on," she says. "In a true sense, it's all I have."

6

The New Woman in the Rectory

The rectory door is opened not by the usual house-keeper, but by a man, who you'd guess was a priest in mufti, and who in fact turns out to be the pastor. But you're not there to see him. You're there to see the associate pastor. The call goes upstairs, and a few minutes later there's a footfall in the hallway, and the associate pastor enters the front parlor. The associate pastor is a woman. It's a hot summer's day in a large city, and it's been a long walk from the train. She asks if you want a can of beer; you settle for ice water.

The associate pastor is a sister, and she has a name. But I can't use it in writing about her, for she ministers in a diocese that does not designate, recognize, tolerate women associate pastors. There are women religious working as she does in parishes of the United States, and most everywhere they must keep a low profile. So it is with her. She offers me a choice of Old Testament names, along with the traditional Mary, by which to identify her. I choose Mary Deborah.

For 23 years Sister Mary Deborah was a teacher in her order's schools in New York, Cheyenne, Milwaukee, and

Minneapolis. She found herself drawn to parish life by observing the strong sense of God in the lives of so many children and families she came in contact with as a teacher. She became fascinated, and determined. "I wanted to work more directly with people in the area of spirituality," she comments. So she went back to school for studies in parish ministry, acquiring a master of divinity degree and a master of theology degree in spirituality. Then she found a parish to hire her; we'll call it St. Peter's. Now she was in a position to make spirituality the focus of her ministry as a woman religious in a traditionally male role.

When Deborah arrived at St. Peter's, there was no defined role for her. So she made a double agenda for herself. She was especially interested in the role of women in the church, and she wanted to work towards identifying a woman's role as a member of a pastoral staff. The people of St. Peter's were wonderful, she says, in helping her in that agenda.

"I can't baptize," she remarks, "but I was one of the persons who started the baptismal program here. I can't anoint, but I have created the liturgy of anointing that we have here annually. I can't work in a hospital quite as a priest does, but I train all of our hospital eucharistic ministers who are responsible for the eucharistic sacramental life of Catholic patients in the hospitals in our parish."

She also works with the parish catechumenate program and on annulments. "In a sense," she says, "the only thing I can't do is to say Mass." Yet she offers liturgical prayers in nursing homes, and many there seem to feel it is Mass for them. And, when St. Peter's holds its periodic reconciliation rites, Deborah has a room by herself. "I talk to those who come to me," she declares, "and they understand that they are not receiving the official sacrament of the church. But many feel reconciled to themselves and to God through talking and praying with me."

It sounds wonderful, and of course it is wonderful that some women at least are able to minister in the new church as does Deborah. But there are frequent moments of hurt—incidents that crop up to remind her that in the eyes of the official church hers is almost a bootleg ministry. For instance she has the title associate pastor, but it cannot be published as such. She is not listed in the *Official Catholic Directory,* the detailed register of Catholic parishes and priests of the United States. In fact she is not described as associate pastor in her own parish bulletin. In some places women pastoral ministers have their titles routinely published in parish bulletins, but not in Deborah's diocese. So St. Peter's deferentially omits all titles from its bulletin, for everyone.

There are other reminders to Deborah that her status is second class. When the annual meetings of diocesan clergy are called, she stays home. And when chancery forms require the signatures of everyone in the house, hers does not appear. As an example, a few years ago the diocese had an evaluation process in which staff and parishioners were asked to rate the work of the pastor. "Well, we did the evaluation," Deborah recalls, "and when it came to the signing of the final document there was space for the pastor, the appointed associate pastors, and 'other.' I refused to sign, because I am not 'other.'" It was a small matter, she adds, but obviously when one shares the work, the joys, and the pain of parish life indignities like this can cut very deeply.

Thus it follows that Deborah feels that the church has

115

dealt her short as a woman, and that Holy Orders should be available to people of her sex. Yet, if Holy Orders were offered to her tomorrow, surprisingly she would probably say no. "I would have to say, 'Not in the way ordination is conceived now.' It would have to be a renewed priesthood. I would not want to have to assume the kind of clerical role that priests do now. It would ruin my work. I don't want to be clerical. I don't think I'm clerical. At least I try not to be."

Inevitably one must wonder why one would in effect want to "play" at being priest—to use a very tendentious verb—when at the same time one is uncertain she would take Holy Orders were they immediately available to her. Deborah's explanation is bound up with her apostolic desire to facilitate the sacramental life of the church for other women and men. "I have chosen to work on the level of the parish," she comments, "because when significant change comes I want some people to be able to say, 'Why not?' Having experienced my ministry—the ministry of a woman—they should be able to say that more easily."

By significant change Deborah is referring of course to a rewriting of Canon Law which would allow women to be ordained, and referring as well to the encouragement and development of new official ministries in the church. "Whichever way significant change comes about," she says, "there will be people who have experienced women's ministries, and the new actuality won't be such a shock to them. People will be able to say, 'Why not have women?'"

In one sense, therefore, Deborah's would be a ministry of gradualism—women coming gradually to the priesthood, much as the vernacular came gradually to the church in the step by step procedure adopted by the bishops after Vatican Council II. But Deborah rejects the notion that she is a gradualist, or some kind of borer from within. "I've chosen my role because it gives me the opportunity to work with people the way I want to," she comments. "Other people work in other ways. They lecture, write books, do research, actively work with feminist groups that challenge church policy and legislation regarding women. I know what I would like to see, and I work in my own way to help bring it about."

Does she expect to see great change in her lifetime? "Well," she says with a smile, "there are women mayors in San Francisco and Chicago and a Polish pope in Rome, and five years ago I would never have thought any of those things possible." So, yes, she has hope. "Sometimes I get discouraged by the entrenchment against women and the backlash when women assert themselves. But there's a God of justice, and there are many good women and men working for justice in the church. So maybe. It will be a very pleasant surprise if significant change comes. If it doesn't, I will have given my life for something that is very important."

In all of this Deborah is cut from a different bolt of cloth from so many New Nuns. And specifically in this sense: She is a woman with many institutional grievances, but nevertheless she is still a woman willing to work within the institution on its basic institutional level. The paradox does not impress her. "I love the church, and I believe in the church," she comments, "and when you want something to change you have to work for it. This is my understanding and why I am willing to work in an institutional setting. I've been hurt by it; I've been wiped out by it. But I've also gained a lot of strength."

The manner in which she is accepted in her parish has

been an enormous personal help. Acceptance has been total. Some parishes of the country have trouble merely accepting women eucharistic ministers; recently, when Deborah returned after a very serious operation, parishioners were so thrilled to see her back that they crossed virtually en masse to her communion line. "I was just overwhelmed," she remarks.

For parish services of a liturgical kind Deborah does not wear any special vestments or distinguishing garb. "I take care to dress appropriately," she remarks. "That is, if it's an informal, casual prayer or liturgical gathering, I dress casually. If it's more formal, I tend to be dressed-up. I wear tailored clothes, and I feel comfortable." She explains that she has never felt the need of an alb or a Roman collar. "I greet people before and after each Sunday liturgy, and I have an established identity that goes beyond any identifying clothes."

If she were to officiate as the principal celebrant at a public liturgy, she says she would find wearing a liturgical robe an appropriate practice. "But I am never the principal celebrant at a public liturgy," she says, "so it hasn't been a consideration for me so far."

Nevertheless this would seem to leave unresolved the difficulty of the stranger arriving, say, at the rectory door, and being greeted by whom? The housekeeper? The parish secretary? The sister in everyday women's clothes could be anyone, and least of all the associate pastor.

Deborah dismisses the problem. "You can make plain who you are when you introduce yourself," she says. "The important thing is the care you give to people, the way you're able to help them; or the way you're just able to be with them, to support them. It's the presence you share with them that counts. That doesn't require any explanations at all."

And so it is that Deborah goes about her work as associate pastor, and there is plenty for her to do. St. Peter's has a heavy quotient of women, perhaps as many as three fourths of its parishioners being female. There are many single women, widows, and divorcees. For a woman minister there is therefore a natural ambience, a built-in corps of supporters. "They're very conscious of the role of women in the world," Deborah says gratefully. So naturally they should be able to identify with women officials in their own church.

There is also a pastor who, in Deborah's words, "understands the need for women in the ministry," and is willing to share the decision making with her. This she finds remarkable because theirs is a diocese where at least until recently a priest must wait until 25 years after ordination to be in line for a pastorate. Many forced to wait that long for the parish post of authority are not always disposed to share decision making with others, and particularly someone whom the church itself does not officially recognize as belonging to the ordained elite. Deborah's pastor is not that type of man. She credits him with being helpful and collegial, and anything but an autocrat.

He is also very unthreatened, although willing to play the survival games forced on people by the chancery. Example. Deborah found herself in hot water at chancery for an incident following in the wake of a statement out of Rome that concerned women. (She asks that I be no more specific about the statement than this.) There was a protest by women, and it extended to several dioceses and involved demonstrations in the cathedrals of those dioceses. To her dismay one television network identified her as the coordinator of the protest nationally. Which she was. She had set up the television people with contacts, but the ground rules were that she was not to be interviewed. Anyway, at what seemed to be the end of the filming the television reporter turned to her and asked what she thought about the statement. She responded impulsively and that night appeared on television screens as the coordinator of the protest. A few days later came a telephone call from chancery: "Is Sister Mary Deborah preaching in your church? . . . Well, she may not." For a whole year Deborah did no preaching, then she quietly returned to the pulpit. She preaches Wednesday mornings, and usually once-a-month on Sundays.

How many women there are in roles like Mary Deborah's across the country is impossible to say. In many dioceses some women work as parish ministers. Generally their role is clearly defined as to what they can do and cannot do. Then there are others like Deborah, who share totally in the ministry of their parish. She is one of five or six so working in her own diocese. There are more across the country—some of whose ministry is a matter of public record; most of whose is not. "It's still a kind of no-man's land," Deborah says, quickly correcting herself to "no-person's" land. "So much depends on the ecclesiology of the priest who's pastor of the parish. If he understands what is happening in the church, if he shares the work and the decision making with the women, then something positive happens," she continues. "There are one or two instances in the United States where a bishop has actually named a woman as associate pastor, but those are rare. It's usually an internal thing within a parish."

A New Woman in the Rectory

The church's resistance to women's ministry is a case of cutting off one's nose to spite one's face, in Deborah's opinion, particularly in view of the male vocations crisis. "They're afraid of women," she says of the church's male leadership. "They don't know how to deal with women. Theirs is a very narrow kind of clerical education, and many of them do not have the skills to work with people."

Deborah does not live in the rectory. She lives in an apartment with another sister about 10 minutes from St. Peter's. Her companion works in a peace and justice center downtown. Deborah maintains strong ties to her religious congregation, but she confesses that she does not spend as much time "serving or caring" for it as she did. "My community is broader based now," she declares.

She has moved away, but she does not look back with regrets. "As a young sister, I was very happy," she reflects. "I loved to teach, and I had marvelous teaching experiences. Then in the late 1950s, early 1960s, I began to read Rahner, Schillebeeckx, and Küng, like everyone else, and I began to realize that the church had to change." She experienced the "thrill" of the initial changes—in the liturgy; in the different ways of regarding apostolate—and she realized that she wanted to know more theology, more Scripture. Something within her said, "Teaching is fine, but now it is time to be more basically involved in the church, working with the people's spirituality," her own included.

She set three goals for herself: "I wanted to change my lifestyle, I wanted to change my ministry, and I wanted to deepen my prayer life. Have I succeeded? My lifestyle is not exactly the way I would like it, but I struggle with it. I aspire to a lifestyle of sharing more with people and of identifying with the poor. Here at St. Peter's our people

121

are for the most part fairly affluent. So I have a lot of questions with myself about that goal. As for the others, my ministry certainly has changed, and I really think I have deepened my prayer life." In other words she has moved on, as well as away.

And as far as she is concerned there can be no going back—to the convent, to the habit, to the traditional apostolates—for her or sisters like her. "There are so many young women and men who can teach and administrate in our schools, who can be nurses and doctors and administrators in our hospitals. Why not leave that for them?" she asks. "I just can't understand using the talent of women, who understand the coming of the kingdom, and the urgency of bringing justice to the world, on work that could be just as well done by other professional people."

The comment sounds harsher than it actually is. Deborah is not being contemptuous or indifferent to those who find a satisfying ministry in the so-called traditional apostolates. Her point is that valuable religious womanpower should not be wasted in areas where there are lay professionals who could do the job just as well, or maybe even better. In other words, though she did not say so herself, she is pleading for a return to the realism that was operative in the 1950s, when lay editors were brought into the Catholic press in new, large numbers, thus releasing priests, particularly on the diocesan level, for work that was more directly related to their priestly training.

Certainly she does not feel that she has abandoned her religious congregation, or work that presumably belongs primarily to women. From the start, she says, she had received nothing but encouragement from her provincial.

Still, she does contribute to a personnel drain, and that

she regrets—except she does feel that smaller religious communities are the wave of the future, and that religious congregations will not flourish numerically in the way they did in the past. Indeed she sees no need for them to, "if we have a large group of lay ministers." But she feels women's religious congregations will nevertheless survive, as they should, in keeping with the rhythms of human relations within the church. "I think we'll always have a need for women's religious communities," she says, "if only because they're independent of the clerical structure of the church. Religious communities often call us as a church to new things. There's a sense of freedom among them, and there's a tremendous tradition of education and ministry of the kind that looks forward with vision. But like everything else, they're going to change a lot. Their role in the church will be more of a prophetic one—and if you look back through history, you'll find they have been prophetic, in many ways."

Obviously large numbers are not needed for prophetic witness. Nor are large numbers needed to help chart new directions. Nor to assess and offer judgment on the work of evangelization in the church. Here there is a lot of room for the nun, new or traditional, to function. "I think religious communities are the key to the development of strong ministerial roles for the laity," she argues. "They will be the strong helpers, to share their religious life and the concerns of ministry."

As for the laity, Deborah brims with hope, and particularly for the new generation of Catholics which in the last 15 years or so has taken quite a different view of religious practice and morality than the generation of their parents.

She is very positive about the church's future in the context of this generation. "Many of them have stepped away from the church," she concedes. "They've been alienated for a period of time. They have to find and internalize the values of religion, and the value of a prayer life and spirituality. But I think they are searching for that."

Those who have stepped away will come back, she predicts—"if there is something to come back to." She offers St. Peter's as an example. "Young people come back all the time. Young families come back. And one of the things they say is, 'We have not found life like this before in the church.' They really want to identify with the church. They want to have a sense of community in the church. They don't want the old conservative hard lines. What they're interested in is hospitality, welcome, and a spirit of community. They come to be a part of us, to help us to create the good human life, supported and strengthened by Christian values."

But how many St. Peter's are there to which the strayers will want to come back? More than one might think, according to Mary Deborah. "There are pockets of new life all over the place," she says. "I have friends all over the country, and they are able to find parishes where there is real life, real concern for the people, real concern about justice and peace—and a real concern for a spirituality based on a theology that recognizes the development of the human being and the power of God in all our lives; in a word, a viable community with large spiritual values."

But then she adds her codicil: This viable community is dependent on the equality of women, and a few things more. "Where you have a church that recognizes women, that is attentive to people with problems in their married lives, that is attentive to people of different lifestyles or different sexual preferences, such as the homosexual, that is caring of people and just doesn't arbitrarily say, 'You're sinful, you're wrong, you're bad'—then you have a church that is a reflection of the Jesus of the Scriptures. That kind of church is possible today," Sister Mary Deborah concludes. "It is what Christianity is all about."

7

Seeding Hope in East Harlem

Each Thanksgiving-time *Village Voice* investigative reporter Jack Newfield shifts gears and writes a piece about heroes unsung who help restore faith in human nature. It's his bromo-seltzer, his cure from the headaches of a year's diet of reporting lost causes, campaign cover-ups, promises reneged upon, and assorted hypocrisies of the humankind on his newspaper beat. Recently he tipped his typewriter keys to Sister Mary Nerney, C.N.D., whom he described as no naive social-worker, but one tough street-smart nun. He couldn't have been more on target.

Nerney is initiator, developer, and presently executive director of Green Hope, a halfway house for women who have no place to go after their release from prison. It's a house that provides temporary lodging, helps women find jobs, tutors in education and nutrition, and, in sum, eases the awesome and sometimes frightening transition to freedom from the world of iron bars, regimentation, and debasement. As for Nerney, in Jack Newfield's words, she spends her days "chasing drug-pushers off her corner, raising funds for the project, meeting with judges and parole officers, and dealing with the local butcher and oil delivery man." That's a mite profuse, but only a mite.

Nerney works in the city where she grew up, but the neighborhood where she was raised and the neighborhood where she works now are worlds apart in everything but geography. Home turf as a youngster in the 1940s, early 1950s was the Washington Heights area—neat, comfortable, middle class. Green Hope turf is East Harlem. Its block looks like a set from the movie "Fort Apache, The Bronx." Even the Catholic church up the street is ringed in tight by an iron fence, as if it were under siege. And here Nerney thrives, motivationally and spiritually. Green Hope headquarters is a converted convent on East 119th Street.

Mary Nerney entered the Sisters of the Congregation of Notre Dame in 1956, and for 11 years was a grade school teacher in New Jersey, Rhode Island, and New York. During 1970-71 she was principal of an inner-city school in New Haven, serving in the main minority students in an individualized approach to education. Meanwhile she was taking special training as a psychologist, and she was subsequently named school psychologist at St. Columba's in New York City. It was then that her new life as a religious began to fall in place.

She became involved with the New York branch of Network, the social-justice lobby centered in Washington that engages the dedication of so many sisters around the country. Criminal justice was one of the priority issues of the New York group, and in 1973 Nerney was asked to organize a conference on the subject. She did this by drawing together as co-sponsors Network, the National Assembly of Women Religious, and the Sisters Council of New York. The conference was held in February, 1974, and one point kept surfacing throughout the meeting: "The needs of women prisoners are the greatest, and they are not being serviced."

Meanwhile Nerney was working with the Clergy Volunteer Program, spending one full day a week at the Women's House of Detention on Rikers Island. She was not there many months before she noted a pattern of recidivism; many of the same people were coming back to jail. Nerney was puzzled, and she probed. In answer to why the recidivism, she kept hearing, "I don't have anywhere to go." "I couldn't find a job." "I drifted back to some of my friends." At the same time she noticed how scared many women were as they left Rikers, and as she tried to find them assistance she quickly learned how few public resources were available to help these women back into the social mainstreams. Small wonder they were scared.

"Women are an invisible part of the prison population," Nerney says indignantly. "They're forgotten. Men in prison are forgotten, too. But women are *really* forgotten because they're a much smaller group of people. There are fewer services available, fewer job opportunities, and fewer training programs. Very often society thinks of the woman who has been in prison as a bad woman, which further discriminates her."

Nerney repeatedly voiced her indignation, saying, "somebody should do something about this," until friends started asking her, "Well, why don't *you* do something?" The challenge put to her, she at first backed off, her response being, "I really don't do that sort of work. I'll gladly help somebody to do it, but it isn't my work." Soon enough, however, it became plain that if the work was ever going to be done, she would have to do it. "I loved my work as school psychologist at St. Columba's," she says, "but my concern was gradually shifting to the needs of women in prison. So I started Green Hope, and many people were very helpful along the way."

She sounds so low-key that one would almost think the challenges were minimal. They were not. She had to secure community approval to start the program; she had to line up the cooperation of the justice system bureaucracy; she had to secure funding; she had to find co-workers; she had to find a building—for Green Hope was hopeless without a roof over its head. This last challenge proved especially fascinating.

As a nun Nerney realized that a convent building was the answer to her housing problem. They have small bedrooms, large common areas, and space available for offices. She figured that, with parochial schools closing and with the sister-drain of recent years, convents must be available. So she went to the Archdiocese of New York for help; she did not receive any, not immediately. The Diocese of Brooklyn did show her available buildings in its precincts, but the buildings were either too small or not appropriate.

She had half an eye on Holy Rosary convent, standing empty on East 119th Street in East Harlem. The building did not need any basic renovations and was in very good condition. It was a relatively new structure, having been built in 1961 and used only until 1973, when it was vacated. The complication was that Archdiocesan Catholic Charities had its eye on the building too, planning to make it into a group home for adolescent girls. But a concession was made. While Catholic Charities was completing its plans, Mary Nerney was allowed to move in, thanks to the intercession downtown of the pastor, Monsignor Victor Pavis. Green Hope was a reality. Nerney had hurdled all the other obstacles to getting started, and now there was a roof overhead. But the stay was only to be temporary; it was only to be for the summer months of 1975. This was nerve-racking, as it meant her search was still on. But the problem soon solved itself. Those working on the Catholic Charities project could not settle on reimbursement rates with the appropriate public agency, and their project was pigeon-holed. Green Hope was permitted to stay. It is still there seven years later.

Green Hope is a residence for women who have no place to go after their release from prison. For some women it is also an alternative to further incarceration, a sort of release/relief station. If the individual does well she will receive probation rather than a sentence. The average stay is four to six months, during which time the ex-offenders begin to pull together the strings of their lives and to become independent. "We assist the women in getting a job or getting into training," says Nerney. "We have classes here in remedial reading and math. We do some drug and alcoholism counseling. We do family counseling; as for women who are mothers, there is the whole question of regaining custody of the children, providing that's what they want. Finally, when individuals are ready to establish their independence, we help them get an apartment, then follow up for as long as the women wish it."

There are no religious litmus tests at Green Hope. The old convent chapel is still there, but it functions now mostly as a quiet room, where individuals can go to think, or reflect—or pray, if they wish. "Sometimes women have asked to have their ministers come in for religious services, but for the most part they go out for services," says Nerney. "This is encouraged, but it is not part of the program." Green Hope, therefore, is not pushing religion, as it were. But it does extend helping hands, and in a sense this is a form of religion to Nerney. "I think of religion in a broad dimension," she remarks, "so therefore everything is religious."

Despite its lack of formal religious ties, Green Hope remains a formidable apostolate, made the more so, the outsider would presume, by the clientele itself. Nerney looks on Green Hope's women as good, decent people in need of help. Which they are. At the same time, however, they are not easy school-truancy cases. These are women with serious felony charges in their background, ranging from petty larceny to homicide. As many as 24 will be at Green Hope at any one time, and these women Nerney has made her life and her apostolate, barring the doors to no one, except the woman with a long psychiatric history. "We do not have a staff that is psychiatrically oriented," Nerney explains, almost apologetically. "We are not a therapeutic community or a hospital setting."

She offers a profile of the average resident: "She would be in her early twenties, and would probably have one, maybe two children. She would not be married. She would probably be black or Hispanic (70 percent are black, and about 17 percent Hispanic). She would probably have been on welfare. She may or may not have had any prior job experience, and she probably does not have her high school diploma."

It is not exactly the appealingly needy type that one finds featured in vocation ads to stir the inquiry of a prospective religious. Yet Nerney is there, and so are two other sisters, from orders other than the Congregation of Notre Dame, to assist and be part of the professional staff. All told, Green Hope has a staff of 14, their work being funded by a variety of government agencies (60 percent), as well as corporations, individuals, and church groups (40 percent). Other than Nerney's being a sister and the building's being a former convent, Green Hope is not church-related. It is a private, nonprofit agency. But if ever an agency were performing a corporal work of mercy, that agency is Green Hope.

Still, is it worth it all in wear, tear, and expense? The question is insulting, because lives are at stake, and because if Nerney had not started this work back in 1975, chances are that no one would be doing it yet. But for the persistent skeptic, there are answers—strong indicators, from both the pragmatic and spiritual viewpoints, that Green Hope is worth every ounce of energy, every grain of dedication that goes into it.

Some time ago Nerney estimated per capita costs of her program at $27 a day, compared to $45 a day cost to taxpayers for each woman held at Rikers Island. That was before the latest rounds of inflation. The cost differential would be even greater today. In addition there are such items as police and court costs, if the individual returned to crime, besides damage caused by the crime itself. Green Hope, in a word, is a bargain public service, a great economy.

It is also a spiritual energizer, as true humanitarian works frequently are for those intimately connected with them. Nerney attests to this. "As a sister, I am happy to share and live my life with the women who come to Green Hope. I feel that I bring a sense of presence, of commitment to people who share my nèed, as I share theirs, for community. In a world of consumerism and materialism, there is a crying need for viable alternatives that value people over things. I hope Green Hope is a step in that direction." It is.

But it is when one gets to the bottom line, to results, that Green Hope really proves its worth. "How many of the women who have gone through the program have returned to prison?" Nerney asks rhetorically. "The recidivism rate here has been very low. That's one successful indicator for the program. The other, and far more important one for me, is the qualitative change the program has had in the life situations of many of the women: that someone has been able to get some training; that someone has been able to get a high-school diploma, or at least a bit closer to one; that someone has been able to get a job and have her own apartment; that someone has worked out the difficulties with her family so she can return home."

For the first three years of the program Mary Nerney lived among the women of Green Hope, along with a co-religious of the Congregation of Notre Dame, Sister Margerita Castenada, who was a volunteer in the program while also teaching at St. Jean Baptiste High School. Because Green Hope is, in effect, a crisis center, with the expected and the unexpected happening 24 hours a day, Nerney found she had to move her bed out, so to speak, if she wanted to get any rest. So right now she lives with a community of Religious of the Sacred Heart, who have a renovated brownstone around the corner of 118th Street. It is within easy walking distance of Green Hope, but it is not a scenic walk, nor one some people would find altogether safe. Nerney dismisses any problem. She feels not only safe in the neighborhood, but "very safe." She is well known up and down the block, particularly by the children. "If you just look at the setting, it certainly could be depressing," she admits. "But if you look at the people, you cannot be depressed, because of their aliveness." She adds that the same aliveness is true of the people at Green Hope. It makes the work easier.

Still, Green Hope is such a constant challenge, and the neighborhood itself is so beat up, that one can imagine the work would wear down the most dedicated person in time. Nerney says her work is a joy, not a chore. Still, she does not rule out a change some day for herself, which is one reason, apart from reasons of organization itself, that she hopes the program does not depend on her availability. She does not believe it does.

"Now, after seven years, there is a basic way that the program functions, and that does not depend on me," she comments. "Program decisions are made for the most part on a team basis. I believe that is an important aspect of the supportive nature of Green Hope. No one need be alone in decision making. Since much of Green Hope involves dealing with crisis, then it is very important that the staff work closely together and be a supportive community. I believe this is true for the wonderful staff at Green Hope."

If she did move on, Nerney is quite certain it would not be to an apostolate in another field. "If I did move on," she declares with emphasis on the conditional, "it would be to respond to a need not now being addressed that would involve women and the criminal justice system." She restates the essential problem: Prisoners are forgotten in so many ways, but especially women, because they are a smaller prison population. Their needs are more complicated, and problems that led to their being in prison in the first place are not being addressed.

Nerney comes down hard on the current criminal justice system. "It is not just," she says. "While some people need to be in 'prison' for a certain time, I do not believe prison should be utilized as it is now—for large numbers of poor people." She believes there are alternatives that fulfill the real issues of community safety and offender-rehabilitation. Of course, for some Green Hope would be one of them, thanks to no one but Mary Nerney.

Mary Nerney does not see "the problems and violence" of the criminal justice system being solved in her lifetime. So her life's work obviously is cut out for her, if not forever at Green Hope, then in some related area of justice for the woman ex-offender. Either way, the societies of church and community can be grateful that busy about the tasks is one who has so directly incorporated into her work-a-day world the law of love as expressed in the Beatitudes.

8

Another Way to be Religious

They are two Sisters of Notre Dame de Namur running a preschool and early-grades school in the Massachusetts North Shore community of Wenham. There are 46 children in the preschool classes; 26 in the first and second grades.

This is a parochial school, right? Wrong.

This is a private Catholic school, right? Wrong.

Notre Dame Children's Class, the institution's corporate name, is not a Catholic school. It is not a parish school. It does not teach religion, nor even assist in the preparation of children of sacramental age for, say, reception of First Holy Communion. The children go to their parish religion class for instruction of that sort—to St. Margaret's, Beverly Farms; St. John's, North Beverly; St. Mary's, Beverly; St. Paul's, Hamilton; St. Joseph's, Ipswich; wherever.

Notre Dame Children's Class specializes in what is called value development, and the sisters in charge—Sister Barbara Beauchamp, S.N.D. and Sister Susan Raymo, S.N.D.—are there with the blessing of their order. In fact their order owns the school, and the two sisters are assigned there.

The school does not fit the traditional model of a parochial school. Barbara Beauchamp makes that plain. "We are two sisters who teach very young children," she exclaims. "We do not teach a 'formal way of religion,' because we do not believe that formal religion can be taught at such an early age. However, we do believe that the basics of all religion can be nourished, nurtured, and built at this early age, and we try to do that."

That's where value development comes in. The sisters stress a system of values through teaching and modeling, and perhaps the latter before the former. "These are very young children," says Beauchamp, "and we attempt to show them how respect is given adult to adult, adult to child, child to child. We teach them to respect the person, respect the environment, respect the value system." The sisters do this through the formation of a triad: children, parents, teachers, all cooperating and interacting, so that all three comprise a learning group, not just the youngsters alone.

"We have assimilated the influence of Montessori philosophy, which believes in the basic potential of every child," explains Susan Raymo. "The traditional parochial school believes in that too, but I think we have actualized it more. Besides, we're not only educating the children; we're working with parents as well." The school has speakers and workshops; the parents are expected to be there.

"The trouble with parochial schools as I knew them," Beauchamp interjects, "is that we met the parents perhaps once every two months, and we met the parents only with a problem. That was it. In our type of school we're meeting the parents daily. We're meeting the parents for lectures. We have them at school for the children's exhibits. We find ways of involving them. Parental participation is a prerequisite at our school. Parents must participate in some way, even if it's only fixing up the playground on Saturday, or teaching some basic Spanish to the children. That interaction, that reciprocity is very important to us. We are sharing the teaching responsibility of parents and parental figures."

But this old parochial-school hand has twinges of skepticism. The sisters talk of value development, and the phrase occurs and reoccurs about teaching respect for the environment and for property. The children, for instance, may use any piece of equipment they want, but they must put it back in place and they may not abuse it. There is an obvious pride that some pieces of equipment in the school are 14 and 15 years old.

But doesn't this give too much importance to property? "We're not teaching respect for property per se," says Beauchamp. "We're teaching respect for the ecological system—taking care of it, being mindful of it. We're not concerned about property for property's sake."

"Let me give you an example," she continues. "Today's *Boston Globe* front page describes the conditions of the streets of Boston. Litter everywhere. Nobody cares. It's just thrown, and the city doesn't have enough people to clean it up. Well, why do we have to have people to clean it up? Where is the respect? You know, if you have a McDonald's bag, you just don't drop it on the street. You find a container to put it in. That's the type of respect I'm talking about."

Beauchamp concedes that this is a secular value rather than a religious one, but she adds that she hopes respect for property will develop into respect for people, and that is a religious value.

Still, the skeptic in me persists. Are not the values of her school—respect for the environment, cooperation, self-esteem, consideration for others, acceptance of differences (Notre Dame has a broad ethnic enrollment)—values that the child would receive in the ordinary parochial school?

The two respond that they are not sure what the ordinary parochial school is today. Beauchamp, a parochial school teacher for nine years, has been out of that work since 1967, when she became co-founder of Notre Dame Children's Class. Much the same with Raymo. She has been on the faculty at Notre Dame for 10 years. She came fresh out of her training as a sister.

Still, they have friends who are sisters and teachers. Can they not surmise from experiences their friends pass on in conversation? Beauchamp gives an answer that dramatizes how much the parochial school has changed since my time in them, the 1930s. "To be perfectly honest," she says, "there aren't many sisters who are teaching today in parochial schools. The teachers are mostly lay persons. In the parochial schools around the North Shore, for instance, there's one sister out of eight lay teachers. That's the situation as it is. Our sisters are not involved in direct teaching in parochial schools as you knew them when you went to school. Our sisters are mostly principals; they're administrative people; they're in guidance; they're CCD coordinators. Today you have very few sisters who are directly involved in the classroom."

One implication of this statement is that the religious content of one's parochial school education is quite different from what it used to be. Beauchamp says this is "definitely" so. Raymo says it would "seem so" from all she hears. But she, for one, is not particularly concerned. "I personally don't think we should teach religion in the confines of a classroom," Raymo comments. "Religion is a way of life, not just the 'icing' on the student. It needs the work of the whole family, the whole unit, to know what religion means in today's world, and how it is supporting of or antithetical to life."

Convinced as both Beauchamp and Raymo are about the importance and effectiveness of their school, neither is certain that the Sisters of Notre Dame de Namur would begin something like it again. This is so even though the school fits into that new concern about the pedagogy of the nonpoor, an interest that has come into focus in some Catholic circles through sociologists like Sister Mary Augusta Neal of the Notre Dame de Namur order. The school in Wenham provides scholarships for families who could not otherwise send their children to the school; it does strive for an economic mix. On the other hand Wenham is anything but a poor area, and inevitably the affluent tend to predominate. Raymo has no apologies for this, or her presence in Notre Dame Children's Class.

"Let me tell you why I'm not in the inner-city with the poor," she remarks. "I came from a poor South Boston background, and I just can't see a way of breaking that poor cycle. I've seen relatives who have had abortions, who have been jailed. The generation is just going further and further down, in my opinion. I don't know how to stop that. It's discouraging to me, and it's discouraging to them. Maybe I'm running away, escaping things. But maybe too I'm helping to change some values on the other end. In order to help the poor you have to work at both ends of the scale. You have to work with the affluent too. And of course you have to work for political changes. I don't know all the answers, but I do know that sisters have been working in South Boston for a hundred years, and we haven't changed it. I think we have to find other ways."

Notre Dame Children's Class is not a money maker, but with tuitions of $800 a year for preschool children and $1200 for children in the first and second grades, it does cover plant and staff expenses on a teacher ratio of one-to-eight in preschool and one-to-thirteen in the primary grades. Nevertheless the sisters are doubtful a project such as theirs would be launched again. Part of the reason would be vocations; for the Sisters of Notre Dame de Namur, as well as other congregations, do not have the numbers they once had. In addition there is the matter of the split several years ago of the Massachusetts Province of the congregation, a happening that no doubt affected the resources and tailored the ambitions of both the new provinces.

The split occurred along ideological lines. The Sisters of Notre Dame de Namur were 1000 in Massachusetts, and, as Raymo explains it, differences cropped up about dress and freedoms. Some of the sisters wanted a more secluded, cloistered life—in other words the old tradition. Others wanted to explore new lifestyles and new roles as ministers. So the Massachusetts Province was split into a Boston Province and an Ipswich Province. Most of the older sisters grouped into the Ipswich Province, and today their median age is about 65. They number some 600. Most of the younger sisters, the 40-ish and younger people, went to the Boston Province. Their re-examination of ministry has taken many of them beyond the classroom—into peace and justice work; into the hospice movement for death and dying; into religious education; into state houses as lobbyists; and other areas of a second ministry. The Boston Province currently numbers about 270 sisters. Two are Barbara Beauchamp and Susan Raymo. They are happy to continue with the work of teaching to which they have been long assigned.

Barbara Beauchamp, born in 1937, has been a Sister of Notre Dame de Namur since 1955; Susan Raymo, born in 1945, has belonged to the order since 1964. They live in a bright, sparkling housing development in Beverly that was initiated by the Archdiocese of Boston, back before stagflation and the New Federalism, when dioceses had more funds than they do now and chose—some of them— to put the funds to work for noninstitutional, general humanitarian purposes. The development is on its own now, and the two sisters are the only Catholic institutional presence there—although they are there in no institutional capacity. Raymo serves as one of the development's nine directors, and the two volunteer in group projects and act as good neighbors to all and sundry. But they shun the sister role, one reason being that they believe it tends to foster old sister-will-do-it, father-will-do-it syndromes.

For instance the sisters pulled back a bit as volunteers on the crafts program for children, because the impulse of the people was to defer to the sisters on matters and let them do everything. Eventually a search committee was organized, and a program director was hired to run the program.

Still, the sisters are there, as good neighbors would be, in times of crisis and emergency. "One apostolic service we perform here is that of listening—listening to people with difficulties," remarks Beauchamp. "Not that we can solve

143

their problems. But we can listen and maybe discern a need or two that we can meet, or ease by directing the individual to another person or agency in a position to help. We have more of an opportunity to do that sort of thing, because we're free. We don't have children. We don't have the financial problems that many of these families have. We are freer to hear what their needs are and maybe respond to them in some small way, even, as I say, if it's only by listening."

Raymo adds that they hope by their lifestyle "to consciously change the image of the sister" that many people seem to carry from their childhood. "How many times have you heard, 'Oh yeah, the sisters of the school. . . .' I'd bet 90 percent of the time the follow-up is, 'They hit me with the ruler, they hit me with the clicker—or the beads.'" There is laughter of the kind one hears when a story is half-fable, half-fact, like those old stories about sisters' warning to girls in patent-leather shoes. "Anyway, today sisters don't hit," says Raymo. "They like to share what they have." She might have added that they like also to give example, and these two sisters do give example of what it means to be a good neighbor in many ways, including the aesthetic; they have flower gardens front and back that would elicit the admiration of the women of the Garden Club in the grandest part of town.

There is no formal chapel in the sisters' living unit, or in the development itself, so as worshiping Catholics the sisters describe themselves as "traveling parishioners" of the North Shore. "We don't belong to any one parish, simply because we haven't found one we like," says Beauchamp. Both she and Raymo complain of bad liturgies and meaningless sermons in most of the parishes of their area. The sermons are a particular point of grievance. "They don't say anything," remarks Raymo." 'God is love.' 'God is peace.' What does that mean to my everyday life? I don't think I'm a great public speaker by any means, but I think I could give a sermon far better than some of these diocesan priests." Thus the two search out churches that offer physical space conducive to meditation. "That's important to me," Beauchamp says, speaking for the two. "The liturgy is out there, but physical space offers me a meditative opportunity that satisfies my needs."

One might conclude from certain of their remarks that a housing development is not particularly conducive to prayer and worship, at least for sisters. Raymo disputes the point, and tells a story: "I was to make my perpetual vows in 1976. Now of course our school doesn't belong to a parish, and we don't belong to a parish, so I had difficulty. Where was I going to hold my vows ceremony? My home parish is a whole different place; all the friends and neighbors have moved away. Anyway, we have a community house here, a clubhouse that anybody can use. It's a big room. So I decided to take my perpetual vows in the clubhouse. The people I live with are here; the people from the school are nearby. So we had the liturgy there, and my sister-friends came, and people of all faiths came. I didn't have a lot of money for food and refreshments, but the people asked, 'What can we do?' They baked cookies and brownies and cakes, and we had something to drink, and it was marvelous."

There's more to the story: "In the Sisters of Notre Dame, when one takes the vows of poverty, chastity, and obedience forever, it is usually just the Sisters of Notre Dame who stand and say, 'We accept you, we support you.'

145

But when I wrote my service, I wanted everyone to stand and say that, because it's not only the sisters who accept and support me, but other people who have woven the threads into my life."

And so it happened that for Susan Raymo's vows ceremony a housing-development clubhouse became a chapel; a vows ceremony became a love feast for people of all faiths; and they all heard a sermon that startled and inspired.

"I had as a theme for the ceremony the idea of life as a weaving," says Raymo, "different people, different colors coming into my life, and the weaving not being finished yet. I had three priest-friends at my vows ceremony, and I love these guys. But I wanted a woman to give the homily. I asked one of our sisters, and she gave a talk on Fruit of the Loom. Imagine. Like underwear. When she told me she was going to do this, I almost died. 'Fruit of the Loom. Underwear. You're going to talk about underwear!' I said. Well, she gave the homily, on how it's woven, the warp and the woof together, and how it makes different colors, shapes, styles in your life. It was just a marvelous homily."

Sisters Barbara Beauchamp and Susan Raymo are not glamour-type New Nuns, busy about ministries that attract reporters and cameras for feature pieces in the media. In a way they are New Nuns more in the conceptional than actional sense.

They are teachers, teachers who have shed the religious garb, of course—and who find it ironic that a trend exists in some places to go back to school uniforms. "We have a high school that is returning to uniforms," Raymo remarks. "The students and the parents met with the sisters, and they said they wanted a form of uniform—a skirt, or blazer, or sweater. I kid the sisters. I ask them what they're going to wear. It's a paradox. The students will be in uniform; the sisters won't."

Nor are these two sisters militants on the issue which is joined for so many New Nuns: ordination of women. Beauchamp feels ordination should not be denied to other women, but it is not something that she would pick for herself. (Her almost off-hand attitude makes the analyst in me wonder if militancy on the subject is not directly bound up with one's personal desire for ordination.) Raymo states that she wishes she had Holy Orders "sometimes," as when a Colombian couple recently asked her to baptize their child. Since any Catholic can baptize in extraordinary circumstances, she could have gone ahead and done the baptizing. The parents would not have minded. But that would have been selfish of her, Raymo explains. "The Baptism has to be registered in a parish church, and that would have been impossible if I did it." So she called in a priest. "Still, I wanted to do it, and why couldn't I have?" she asks. The words do not, however, burn with resentment. She is happy in her role. So is her colleague.

In that the two are typical of those thousands of nuns who escape categorizing, as New or Old, and who evidence by mind and work that the work of the sisterhoods will go on, whatever the current ideological battlegrounds. Barbara Beauchamp and Susan Raymo are not above ideology. They have their strong opinions on issue after issue. But there is also the everyday work of the Lord to be done. This they are about, everyday.

9

Keeping the New Church New

Sister Rea McDonnell, S.S.N.D. is a New Nun helping keep the New Church ever new. She functions on educational and theological levels, as director of continuing education at Washington Theological Union in Silver Spring, Md., just beyond the District of Columbia. Her post there is a crucial one.

Washington Theological Union is a Catholic graduate school, which brings together a variety of people and religious orders in a sometimes novel, determinedly renewed-church learning experience. Eight religious men's organizations own the Union; about 30 small orders of men send their seminarians there and some 20 women's communities. Their people are working in the main for master of arts or master of theology degrees. There are also lay people studying for degrees.

McDonnell's responsibilities do not extend to them. Her work is with those who are not in the degree program. It is with people who are on sabbatical, and who have come to the Union to recoup, as it were, or to seek theological and scriptural update. It is with people who are anxious to enter a second ministry: the parish priest, who now wishes to specialize in hospital chaplaincy; the religious brother who refuses to be the servant class in his religious congregation any longer; the veteran sister who does not have a bachelor's degree and who is looking for a little theology. It is with the young person entering religious life who does not have a strong foundation in Catholic tradition. It is even for the young postulant or novice who might not know, for example, how many sacraments there are!

Yes, such people exist, McDonnell confirms, particularly among those under age 25. Part of the reason, she speculates, is that not as many young Catholics are passing through parochial school as before. But more particularly she thinks the reason is that recent generations of Catholic parents have defaulted on responsibilities which should be theirs to transmit the faith. She illustrates the point by telling of a 22-year-old woman, whose only religious education was whatever her grandmother had taught her. "Now she's not a convert," says McDonnell. "She's a born Catholic." The Union can salvage this person, but McDonnell wonders how many vocations, to say nothing of souls, are being lost because so many Catholics are now settling for baptized, but religiously untutored and unchurched daughters and sons. She is glad that at one level she is helping to combat religious illiteracy.

She is glad, too, that as administrator of Washington Theological Union's theology for religious program, and through involvement in the Union's ministries development program, she is able to facilitate second careers for individuals whose apostolic and emotional impulses prod them to move on, notably those who for years have been neglected members of their religious communities. She cites religious brothers as a case in point, particularly in mixed communities comprising priests and brothers both, as distinct from communities made up entirely of brothers, as the Christian Brothers or the Xaverian Brothers. Large numbers are exploring new roles for themselves in the church, and McDonnell finds this not only a proper personal adjustment, but also an important historical rectification. "The first monks were all brothers," she comments. "The monastic tradition was founded on brothers. Priests came later." Result: Except in those orders which took pains to assure position and status for brothers, priests quickly enjoyed the ascendancy, and brothers slipped gradually into secondary or, worse, inferior roles.

"Well now," says McDonnell, "brothers in middle age, who may have been driving a tractor or cooking in a retreat house, are saying, 'You know, I don't derive a whole lot of satisfaction from driving a tractor or cooking anymore. There are community needs out there, particularly in the parishes.' Or they're saying, 'I want to be a benefit to the elderly; I want to take Communion and minister to shut-ins; or I want to visit the hospitals and be certified as chaplain.' These people are coming to school here, and it's good for them and for their orders." (For those going into hospital work, Washington Theological Union is empowered by the United States bishops to issue National Association of Catholic Chaplains' certification.)

Sisters and lay people are similarly finding their way to Washington Theological Union, and the Union is responding, reassuring them about the roles that prospectively are theirs in the church, and training them to assume leadership. The focus is strong on religious women, and there is no timidness about speaking of them as prophets in their own right. "The way in which I think religious women will best assume a prophetic role," says McDonnell, "is by becoming so steeped in the word of God that they begin to discern with a new kind of wisdom, and speak with a new kind of power. They can have big names, like Sister Theresa Kane, or they can be second-grade teachers." Washington Theological Union is steeping people in the word of God.

Rea McDonnell was born in Chicago in 1942 and joined the School Sisters of Notre Dame in 1959. She was a grade school and high school teacher in Chicago and Milwaukee for several years; then she taught Scripture on the college level at Marquette and Boston Universities. She is a lettered woman, holding a master of arts degree in theology from St. John's University in Collegeville, and a doctor of philosophy degree in Scripture from Boston University. She is cerebral but a person with definite emotional tugs back to younger days as a teacher in Chicago's inner-city. "Here at the Union, working with priests, sisters, and brothers, I find it almost impossible to measure their learning processes," she remarks. "In the inner-city, I was able to take a girl, a freshman in high school, 14 years old, reading on the second-grade level, and by the end of the year I could have her reading at eighth-grade level. I could really watch the girls grapple with Christian values, as they are lived out on the streets. I could really listen as they verbalized their decision-making processes. All that was extremely satisfying."

Her experience in the inner-city makes her hope for the survival of the parochial school, particularly in inner-city situations. "I'm not for shutting down the parochial school system," she declares. "I left it because I just wanted to study more." She returns to the Chicago experience: "I spent my last three years of high-school teaching instructing girls who would have been thrown into the jungles of the public schools had their parents not made significant sacrifices to send them to a Catholic school, where we stayed with them until they truly learned to read and write. We stood on our heads, and they responded beautifully. Catholic schools are badly needed there for the basics of education. We are training children in them to be efficient human beings and Christians, and self-determining citizens." Obviously she feels it's very important to keep these schools open.

Today McDonnell is a long way from the inner-city, living in suburban Washington in an apartment with another sister. But she is not so far away from the inner-city that she cannot get back. She does so on Sundays, often driving 40 minutes to St. Benedict the Moor parish in Washington for a two-hour liturgy that for the 300 or so worshipers includes Gospel choir, dialogue homily, and an exchange of signs of peace that lasts about 20 minutes. At St. Benedict's Rea McDonnell says she finds "real community."

"I must admit that daily Eucharist has become a real sore spot for me because of clericalism," she comments. "Sunday Eucharist is still important. But if I don't have a community with whom to celebrate, I would just as soon not celebrate." The clericalism of the American church so bothers her, in fact, that it seems impossible for her to suppress the thought of further, even more dramatic evolutions in her life.

"Right now I am very happy to work with priests," she remarks. "I see many of them shedding clericalism and encouraging the laity more in their gifts. I would particularly like to help priests grapple with understanding issues of social justice, so they could better enable lay people to carry their kind of leaven into political areas."

But there's the larger reality: those priests with whom she finds it difficult to work because of their clericalism. It would seem they comprise the majority of the American clergy. And then there is the reality of America itself. "How long I will be able to stand the pain of a clericalized church in this First World country is a question I ask myself a lot," she states bluntly. "I remember saying a few years back that if the United States goes to war over oil in the Arabian gulf, I am leaving the United States. I just shall not be part of an exercise in exploitation of that sort. But in the meantime I've been reading much on prophets, and prophets stay in their country and keep screaming at the powers that be. Well, I can see myself in that role for a while—hacking away at unjust structures."

McDonnell's big complaint with a clericalized church is that it vitiates justice for women, and for lay people in general. So what will happen when she reaches the point where she cannot stand clericalism any longer? Where is she going to go? What is she going to do? She's thought about all that. "The option is open to go to Latin America," she comments, "where I would be more identified with the poor, and where I could function as a priest. I have no doubt that I am called to priesthood, and I know that women are functioning as pastors and celebrating sacraments as well in Latin America. They just aren't officially called priests. But I don't have to be officially called anything in order to function as I think I should."

Her rationale for a women's priesthood in Latin America, or elsewhere for that matter, is based on the twin elements of right and justice—for the women ministers, to be sure; but also for the individual lay Catholic, male and female. "One thing strong in my consciousness, primarily because of the teaching of the Latin American bishops, is that Catholics have a right to the Eucharist," she explains. "If in many countries of the world Catholics are not allowed the Eucharist except maybe once or twice a year, when a male priest is available, then we are doing an injustice to those Catholics. Pius X said that the Eucharist is the source and center of all Christian living. How can it be for millions, if the Eucharist is only celebrated once or twice a year for them?"

She speaks with the conviction of a woman who could be laying out the blueprint of her tomorrow.

Much as anything else it is new understandings of the traditional vows of religious life—chastity, obedience, and poverty—that have determined McDonnell's life as a nun in the modern world. These understandings have changed markedly since the early 1960s.

As for chastity, there is the discovery, she says, that it is not a virtue so much as it is a gift, God's gift—the gift of celibacy, which some are given for the sake of the Kingdom. "Basically, we religious are focused now on *how* to love, and *how* to love well, as a result of meditation on what vows mean," Rea McDonnell declares. "The vow of chastity used to mean the absence of sex, perfume, make-up. We've moved away from externals to ask how we can grow more free, less frightened of our being women, so that all the gifts of womanhood can be at the service of the church. There is a real desire in so many of the men and women in celibate life to grow in the ability to love well, and that is the inner core of that gift of chastity. Again, it is God's gift, not our achievement."

Concerning obedience, she finds new understandings bound up with the cooperative/consensus modes by which individuals in religious life now generally relate with other sisters, including their provincial. It works just fine for her. "I know I need somebody—my community, my provincial—to take seriously my vision of church and world," she comments. "I expect my provincial and my community to challenge me to examine my gifts and my energy. That is the kind of interaction that obedience is now all about. My provincial has delighted me because she has shown her leadership on social issues. And I need a leader. That doesn't mean that I need someone to hold my hand or give me approval for everything I do. Rather I need—we all need—someone with a vision of church and world, and our place in them, who can point different directions."

Finally poverty. "We used to say that poverty freed us from care about material things. I don't really agree with that anymore. I find that in the United States we have a very capitalistic, greedy, self-serving, materialistic society. And if I deprive myself of creature comforts—and I do try to do that—it is to stand in a kind of counterculture position against the lifestyle that I find so prevalent. I don't want to be a consumer. I want to feel in my body what it's like for people, particularly in the Third World, to be homeless, or deprived, or physically hungry. Solidarity with the poor and a counterculture stance are what I consider the basis of the vow of poverty for me today."

McDonnell welcomes the new understandings of the vows of religious life, for she finds she is freer now to act—

and in a world where action is invited in ways it wasn't always in the past. "For one thing I can take political risks. I can march on the Pentagon, as I have, and if I am thrown in jail, as a celibate, as one in the vow of poverty, I am not depriving my family of my presence, my salary, or whatever."

That's a familiar rationale, but hitherto one heard it only from priests. Only in an age of feminism arrived could one expect to hear it from a nun.

McDonnell is positive about the future of religious life. "It will endure, sure," she says. "Religious life is not a higher way, or a better way. Nor is sex bad. But celibacy does free people to move, and moving and mission will be more urgent in the years ahead." Nevertheless survival will involve the birth of new forms of religious life, she is convinced. She envisions, for instance, smaller communities—groups of celibates, living together or coming together at regular intervals to pray and to plan strategy for helping the Spirit in a constantly changing society. Groups like the one she belongs to in the Washington area. Hers is a group of six School Sisters of Notre Dame, most of whom live alone and meet at least every two weeks to pray together, have dinner, and talk and plan on a variety of levels. They call themselves the Community Without Walls.

"We need to plan strategy," McDonnell says. "For example, how can the political force, which is religious women, move as a bloc on the El Salvador question? One of our group has organized a letter-writing party for concerned sisters of the area, so we can bombard Congress with mail. She's a part of the lobby group Network, as am I." McDonnell sees groups of celibate women, and men, continuing to come together for that kind of service, and she is firmly convinced that women will be up to the tasks confronting a concerned social conscience.

"I think the El Salvador women—the four who gave their lives in December, 1980—challenged lay women and religious alike to look again at their prophetic role," she comments. "Theresa Kane, speaking to the Pope at the Shrine of the Immaculate Conception, gave me such a thrill of hope that religious will reclaim their prophetic role in the church. The initiative is ours for the seizing." She's not worried about authorities' clamping down on religious women. "There's nothing anyone can do really to hurt us, or deprive us of status or function, since religious women have a very low status and function anyway in our male-dominated church." She tells of a friend working in a ministry disapproved of by a particular archbishop. The archbishop wrote to her provincial, saying, "I want you to take away her faculties." This was an order causing great hilarity among the sisters, for of course a nun does not have "faculties" in the sense a priest does. "Does he mean, take away her mind and will?" went the sisters' rejoinder. McDonnell adds, "There's nothing really that can keep my friend from doing the work of the Spirit among a very outcast people." She implies this is a rule for wider application.

And that's what Sister Theresa Kane is reminding religious women of, McDonnell argues: the courage and the freedom to act on their own as sisters, and to speak the word of God, wherever it's called for—not only the word of challenge that Theresa Kane issued before the Pope, but the word of comfort that Rea's own friend issues daily to outcast, minority groups.

"The key is the Scripture," McDonnell concludes. "I've studied the Latin American situation, and I am convinced that the Medellin and Pueblo documents, and all the base-community movements, stem in fact from the Brazilian bishops' and priests' putting Scripture into the hands of the common people beginning around 1945. Scripture is a real revolutionary force. Somehow, as St. John's Gospel says, when we get to make our home in the word of God, we know truth—and truth sets us free to speak and act with the courage of *our* convictions, with the courage of *God's* convictions."

It is apparent from her every word that Rea McDonnell is talking of a sisterhood that itself is becoming revolutionary force: the sisterhood of religious women.

Part III

Phenomenon or Permanent Fixture?

Recently I was talking with a sister who was off on a 500-mile drive early the next day to her home in Maryland. It was a Saturday night, and she said she would be up and away by 6 a.m. "What will you do about Mass?" I inquired, knowing how seriously she took the Sunday obligation, and anticipating I would be told that she had already attended the Saturday evening liturgy.

"I'm picking up a passenger in New York around 11," she responded. "He's a priest-friend, and we'll have a car liturgy along the way."

I thought I was being put on. "A car liturgy?" I said.

"Sure. They're great. We have them all the time," the sister commented. "I love them. They're so reflective of the age, of a church on the move: Mass in a car speeding along the highway. It all seems so natural."

I didn't ask how an open bottle of wine squared with the open-container laws that most states have. I thought rather about the car rosaries and how popular they were back in the 1950s, and obliquely conceded the point that cars can be places of prayer.

I do not expect the car liturgy will ever catch on the way

the car rosary did (for a time). Yet if anything seemed to capture the image of the New Nun, it was the logic that made the car liturgy so attractive to my friend. A pilgrim church on the move; sisters on the move. A new style for a new times. But a new person, too? Well, not exactly.

I tested the point with Sister Marjorie Tuite, O.P., of Chicago, national coordinator of the National Assembly of Women Religious and citizen-action person for Church Women United. "The New Nun is really not *new*," she said. "Rather she is a woman who has chosen to be a member of a religious congregation and as such is in continuity with history. She, with others, has taken seriously the request of Vatican II to examine her own life in the light of the signs of the times in order to respond more effectively to the needs of a complex, technical world. She stands firmly within the faith tradition of which she is a part, the social reality in which she lives, and the historical rootedness of her congregation."

Where then does the New Nun's creative energy come from?

"It comes out of a belief system that is centered in the dignity of the human person," Tuite responded. "She relates to women of the past, women in Scripture, the Old and the New Testaments, women who were foundresses of her congregations, such as Catherine McAuley, Elizabeth Seton, Catherine of Siena. And she relates to the women who touch her life experience day to day, her peers. Because she has struggled with her own self-definition as a woman, as a nun, she easily identifies with those who seek to determine their own lives and free themselves from oppressive structures in church and society. Hence, advocacy for the powerless is central to her ministerial response. She understands the religious congregation as a place in which to find support and evaluation for what she is about. She rejects role as an end and refuses to conform to the stereotypes of what others have in mind she should be. For her working alone is never as effective as working collectively with those who share a similar vision, commitment, and history. Fidelity to the mission of Jesus is deep within her being. Her spirituality is an integration of reflective prayer and action, as she searches to touch transcendence, to respond more fully to the Jesus who lived in history, and to respect the presence of the Spirit within each person."

As for her choice of lifestyle and work place, Tuite remarks that they "are made within the framework of a deepening commitment to the poor."

If there is a composite profile of the women who speak in this book, Marjorie Tuite has provided it. The New Nun is an inspiring person, totally dedicated, and committed in ways that have turned what could be the worst of times for the sisterhoods into, if not the brightest, then the most stimulating. There has been a deep personnel drain. There is difficulty in finding new recruits. These and other problems cannot be minimized. Still, the sisters who have stuck have displayed an apostolic imaginativeness that in many instances has more than made up for the loss of numbers. The sisterhoods are smaller, but more vital than ever.

Even so, the question must be asked: Is the New Nun mere phenomenon or a permanent part of the church's future?

The fairer question might be: Will the sisterhoods survive? In the late 1960s, when the exodus from religious congregations was at almost epidemic levels, it was relatively easy to argue that women religious were a phenomenon that had lasted several hundred years (a short span in the history of the church), and that the sisters were now taking their place in archival pages alongside the parroting priest of the Middle Ages, who was ordained solely to stand at an altar and celebrate Mass continuously in order to discharge a monastery's or order's obligations to donors. However, in the light of more recent history and the endurance of that core of womanhood anxious to make a full-time commitment to the work of the Gospel and the plight of the poor and the powerless, it seems virtually certain that the sisterhoods will survive. As several of the sisters have commented in these pages, their numbers will never be so strong as in the past. But the sisterhoods will survive. The New Nun, if not *the* key to that survival, will certainly be *an* element in it. For in fashioning a new role for the modern woman religious the New Nun has more than established a novel type of sister. She has performed a liberating function. Never again will the sister be a captive of the convent, a handmaiden in a hierarchical system. She has won her autonomy as a person and as an apostolic spirit alert to the demands of social justice, the beckonings of the Beatitudes, and the call to the spiritual and corporal works of mercy.

Will this woman religious be a permanent fixture of church history? Surprisingly the answer to that question does not seem to be an overriding preoccupation with the New Nun. As Tuite said, "If you set us in the context of the signs of the times, we live in this moment of history, and if this moment of history is indeed a moment, then so be it. It's a moment. Permanence is not our concern. We have to create our own history in a context that is both historical and existential."

Obviously the male church has on its hands quite a different woman religious from what it has known. It is a woman who is apostolically individualistic, who has moved from dependency to autonomy, who knows not docileness, and who as far as the internal church is concerned intends to persist until the last vestiges of sexism are routed out, right up to the priesthood. It may be forever until the church has its true Pope Joan, but it will not be long before it has its Father Joans. The anonymous "woman priest" featured in the July 17, 1981 issue of the *National Catholic Reporter* is not unique to herself. Women are being called to the priesthood in the United States by their faith communities, and the tomorrow is not far away when the church itself will be officially calling them. The steps are already being taken. Women are functioning as lectors, commentators, preachers, eucharistic ministers. They are ministering in parishes as assistant or associate pastors. They head up diocesan departments, and not just school departments; one or two dioceses have diocesan chancellors who are women. Women are teaching in seminaries, giving retreats, acting as spiritual counselors. Is it likely that everything will be possible to women in the church except ordination? It seems extremely doubtful.

Indeed, if one applies Rynne's Law, as outlined by Father Francis X. Murphy, C.SS.R., in his book *The Papacy Today*, the church has already changed its mind on women priests. According to Rynne's Law, when the church is about to accept a mutation in doctrinal explanation or disciplinary directive, the whole edifice of tradition draws itself up and refuses to acknowledge the possibility of change. Then with the publication of a papal or hierarchical document that expresses a refusal to budge on the issue, unwitting acknowledgment has been made that the turnabout is already in process. The Vatican's 1977 document "On the Question of the Admission of Women to the Ministerial Priesthood" and Pope John Paul II's remarks in Philadelphia in 1979, one as explicit as the other in rejecting the eligibility of women to become priests, would be indicators under Rynne's Law that the process of change is quite advanced.

There will be officially ordained women priests, although the resistance to the idea is such in Rome that other seeming impossibilities may first come to pass, such as the reactivation in the formal ministry of priests who have married. It is doubtful that the future of the sisterhoods is contingent upon the availability or the option or ordination for women, but it is quite possible that the integrity and integralness of the church as a human and divine institution depends upon full sacramental equality for women. For this is an issue of human and social justice as real as any other.

Meanwhile there are the social issues of the 1980s and what Marjorie Tuite describes as the "groaning" questions: Who lives; who dies; who has shelter; who wanders; who eats; who is free; who is imprisoned; who is enslaved? On all such questions as these, the New Nun is called to prophetic witness. Will she respond? The answer to that is simple. She is responding. Tuite stresses the point in summarizing the manner and mode of today's sister:

"We are women of tough love. Our prophetic consciousness is collective and comes from our history as women and our lived experience. We claim the past but do not rest in the security of the present; so we risk to create a future yet to be. We believe that the personal is political; we work to exercise collective leadership. We stress social justice; we reject institutional loyalty. There is sorrow in our anger. There is conviction in our word. The political consequence of our belief in the dignity of the human person is to argue that every social system in its political, legal, economic, and religious aspects is subject to our critique and to change. We speak a new symbol, a new energy, a new way. We reject privatism as a way of life. Compassion, for us, is to get beyond our own skins and view life from the perspective of the other—for us, the poor. We are committed to struggle that others are empowered to determine their own destiny. 'They' tell us, serve the law that has been handed down. And our reply: *See we are doing something new; even now it comes to light, can you not see it?"*